MYRON STA

GUIDE TO GREEK DRAMA

City-State Press

Guide To Greek Drama

City-State Press

ISBN 0-9709265-2-9

About the Author

Dr. Myron Stagman, an American from Chicago and later San Francisco, was fascinated with Classical Greece since elementary school when reading of Marathon and Thermopylae, Pericles and Socrates, and especially about Athens' fabled Democracy. With a doctorate in English Literature, he became a Shakespearean scholar and a research scholar as well in the Greek Classics.

His often-stated goal: to communicate the essence of the Greek and Shakespearean classics to a general audience, to foster an understanding and appreciation of this wonderful heritage.

Other Works by the Author:

100 Prophecies of the Delphic Oracle
[Prophetic Advice from the God Apollo]

The prophecies, aside from their mystery and marvel, offer an ideal opportunity to describe the extraordinary culture and history of Ancient Greece.

The Athenian Acropolis
&
its Golden Age Background

The Acropolis is not simply monuments. It reflects the magnificent civilization of Classical Athens, its cultural achievements, personalities, living history.

The Burlesque Comedies of Aristophanes

5 essays on Classical Athens (on Democracy, Slavery, Sex, God, and War) provide vital background information to blow-by-blow descriptions of the eleven surviving bawdy, cutting, ultra-democratic plays of the comedy genius.

Shakespeare's Greek Drama Secret

The revelation of Shakespeare's mastery of Greek Drama discloses for the first time this decisive influence on his work.   (in Greek translation)

The **Shakespeare-in-Essence** Series:
the essence of the dialogue interspersed
with brief comments for comprehension
of Shakespeare's deeper meanings

Shakespeare-in-Essence: *Four Monumental Tragedies*
Macbeth
Hamlet
King Lear
Julius Caesar

Shakespeare-in-Essence: *Seven Comedies About Love*
A Midsummer Night's Dream
As You Like It
The Taming of the Shrew
The Merry Wives of Windsor
Much Ado About Nothing
Twelfth Night
The Winter's Tale

Shakespeare-in-Essence: *Three Tragedies of Love*
Romeo and Juliet
Othello
Antony and Cleopatra

Guide to Shakespeare
an introduction to all of Shakespeare's plays:
brief narrations of the story, highlights,
deeper meanings

TABLE OF CONTENTS

INTRODUCTION

The 44 surviving plays of Greek Tragedy and Comedy comprise the most resplendent dramatic tradition in Literature prior to the time of Shakespeare 2,000 years later. Greek Drama was light-years ahead of any rival and all rivals combined. Along with Greek philosophy and political democracy, Greek Drama resided at the summit of the Achievement of Classical Greece, that Golden Era in world history.

Greek Drama was **Athenian** drama, flower of the city-state democracy of fifth century BC Athens. So little of that voluminous, accomplished tradition has come down to us. Yet we may give thanks for those 44 complete tragedies and comedies which are extant. They constitute works of the 4 greatest playwrights of the ancient world -- Aeschylus, Sophocles, Euripides, Aristophanes.

The greatness of Greek Drama can bear comparison with any corpus of drama anywhere in the world. It stands as tall as the Accomplishment of the immortal Shakespeare himself. Indeed, the genii Marlowe and Shakespeare and the other Renaissance prodigies could only arise with the Athenian dramatic tradition there to teach and guide them. That was part of the process we call the Renaissance, those amazing developments in the middle of the second millenium which drew upon the learning of classical Greece and Rome. (The finest achievement of Rome was the preservation of Greek learning; the knowledge, attitudes and techniques upon which Rome depended for its own intellect.)

Greek drama was poetic drama, dialogue composed in verse. In part this accounts for the beauty of the language. (The beauty of Shakespeare's language depends also, in important part, for having been written in poetic verse – just one of the many debts the Renaissance playwrights owed to Aeschylus, Sophocles, Euripides and Aristophanes.)

Greek drama was suffused with philosophic and moral concerns. Thus, it was closely related to Greek Philosophy. (As a symbol of this, Socrates would walk 5 miles to view a play by Euripides – and 5 miles back to Athens from the port of Piraeus.)

Greek Tragedy and Greek Comedy were closely related also to issues of current importance to the Athenian city-state. Indeed the plays frequently acted as comments upon social and political problems.

The Athenians possessed a strong sense of community and love of their city-state. This helped motivate the playwrights to ascend the heights of dramatic excellence.

I sincerely recommend to my readers, read at least the most famous of the works of Greek Drama. *Prometheus Bound* by Aeschylus. The *Oresteia* trilogy by Aeschylus. Sophocles' *Oedipus Rex* and his *Antigone*. (Every tragedy by Sophocles is exquisite.) *Medea, The Bacchae, Iphigenia in Aulis, Hippolytus, The Trojan Women* – all tragedies by Euripides. His dark satire on the Trojan War, (adapted from a chapter in Homer's *Iliad), Rhesus,* is outstanding. For comic delight: *Alcestis, The Cyclops.*

And Aristophanes: the notorious *Clouds* (about Socrates) and the not-famous but merely marvellous *Plutus.* Finally, every modern woman should read *Lysistrata.*

AESCHYLUS

The Father of Western Tragedy

circa
(525-456 BC)

Formal competition between tragic poets took place in Athens at the annual festival of the Great Dionysia from about 530 BC. Thespis (hence the English word 'thespian') was awarded the prize.

The true creator, however, of Greek Tragedy would fight bravely in the wars against Persia, then become one of the finest playwrights in literary history – Aeschylus. His plays featured dialogue, reducing the role of the chorus while adding a second and, later, a third actor. With Aeschylus, drama became not only fully developed but indeed superlative. To posterity's good fortune, the *Oresteia* trilogy and *Prometheus Bound* are among them.

. In the Dionysian festival, a committee chose three tragedians to compete. Each produced a tetralogy, three tragedies followed by a satyr-play comedy. The tragic trilogy, or all four plays, might have a unifying theme, although it was always permissible to do otherwise. Aeschylus commonly developed a unifying theme, the *Oresteia* being the only Greek trilogy left to us.

The drama of Aeschylus should be understood against the historical background within which he was writing. The Persian empire, Greek despots, revolutions and the startling phenomenon of emergent democracy in Greece, the beginnings of the Athenian empire – these were forces and exciting events all directly experienced by Aeschylus.

He was born in Eleusis some twelve miles from Athens. For the first fifteen years of his life he was a subject of the tyrant Hippias whose army was defeated by Sparta. Hippias fled, and eventually found his way to the court of Darius. Nearly twenty years later, the deposed tyrant accompanied the Persian invasion of Greece.

One of the most pivotal battles in history occurred on the plain of Marathon in 490 BC. It was an Athenian victory; for the first time Greeks had beaten an Imperial army. Aeschylus fought at Marathon.

Ten years later, the Persians mounted another and much greater invasion. Emperor Xerxes personally led the Army and Armada. After finally overwhelming the 300 Spartans in a narrow pass at Thermopylae, the Persian land force marched on Athens while the vast Armada sailed to the same destination.

The Athenian leader Themistocles, at the height of the crisis, ordered an evacuation of the city, the populace taking refuge on their ships and on the island of Salamis. The Persians sacked Athens, then marshalled the Armada to overwhelm the heavily outnumbered Athenian ships.

The great Persian fleet encountered keen Athenian seamanship, tactical acumen, and morale, the Greeks winning a spectacular, decisive victory at Salamis in the year 480 BC, after which allied Greek forces beat the Persian army on land at Plataea the following year. From then on, the Greek city-states would be free from the Asian power, and Athenian democracy would prosper and establish a model for other states. Athens would become the leading Greek state and extend her influence into empire. Aeschylus fought at Salamis.[1]

With the advent of democracy, the rights and civic responsibility of the male citizen expanded dramatically. The People controlled and operated the government,

---

[1] Unsung heroes, not only of the battle of Salamis but of Athens' decades-long military strength, included its teams of highly-skilled rowers.

legislated and judged by majority vote. Discussion of public issues occupied much of their time since they were personally responsible for the welfare of their country. Greek Drama often provided social-political comment, and an Aeschylean play has symbolic significance in this regard.

Aeschylus was an idealist, and his art carries moral force. His themes and diction are august, exploring with "brooding grandeur" concepts of Justice, Freedom, Democracy and Tyranny, Peace and War, Unity and Division, Ethics as a universal historic principle. Democracy was indeed "the inspiration of his art". He was deeply concerned with moral causation, insistent about the relationship between sin and retribution, between virtue and happiness. Aeschylus has been called "the most Hebraic of the Hellenes".

This first great playwright concerned himself also with the inferior status of women in Athenian society. His play *The Suppliant Maidens* conveys the unethical and potentially dangerous nature of the problem. Queen Clytemnestra of the *Oresteia* may have been intended to express a similar message. Be that as it may, Clytemnestra is one of the finest female characterizations in Literature.

Aeschylus' use of metaphoric language was superb and highly sophisticated. Not until Shakespeare would another dramatist so weave and interweave a plethora of metaphoric imagery to underlie the surface story and stress its themes.

Moreover, Aeschylus complemented the majesty of his conceptions with extraordinary stage effects. His plays could be picturesque with horse-drawn chariots, a multitude of attendants, much visual symbolism, splendid costumes, a second chorus, innovative choral dances. The masks and attire of the chorus of Furies in the *Eumenides* genuinely terrified people in the audience. Aeschylus acted in his own plays.

At the time of his death in 456 BC, Athenian democracy was functioning smoothly; Athens was the paramount city-state in Greece; and the city's drama and art were unparalleled. Aeschylean idealism and optimism for the world's future seemed well justified. The tomb of Aeschylus became a place of pilgrimage.

A Note on Organization
of the Plays in this Chapter

They are arranged in chronological order by date of composition.

THE SUPPLIANT MAIDENS   date uncertain

Aeschylus' tragedy is perhaps the first extant drama in Western European literature.

"Although I am the King,
I have sworn to do nothing
except after taking
counsel with my people." --
the democratic king,
Pelasgus, to the
suppliant maidens

Alternate title: Latin, *Supplices*. Note that the title of the play ought simply to be *The Suppliants*. But we distinguish between this play and Euripides' drama by the same name via the longer, more closely descriptive title, *Suppliant Maidens*.

DRAMATIS PERSONAE

Danaus, father of the 50 Danaids
Pelasgus, king of Argos
An Egyptian Herald
Chorus of the Daughters of Danaus

The Suppliant Maidens

This was likely the first part of a trilogy, although it may have been the second part. Extraordinarily, the protagonist is a Chorus of 50 young women who are sisters, the daughters of Danaus. And Egyptians at that. Danaus and the maidens have fled Egypt by boat and come to Greece (Argos) for rescue. They were being forced to marry against their wills, and prefer to give up their families and country, and risk their very lives, to escape bondage. Upper-class women in Athens seldom had a choice in the matter, hence Aeschylus' tragedy has a strongly, rebelliously feminist theme.

The author sympathizes with these young women, portraying them as courageous and daring in a male-dominated environment. The prospective bridegrooms, who are warriors, follow them over the sea. The Chorus supplicates the king of Argos, Pelasgus, to protect them.

King Pelasgus personifies the Greek ideal of a democratic king. He wishes to help the maidens – to protect the weak – but feels he must have popular support, and gets it. The play ends with the landing of the Egyptian force which threatens Pelasgus if the women are not handed over. The King stands ready to fight for the Suppliants.

I wish we had the sequel, which has been lost. We do know, or can surmise, something of its contents. The Egyptians conquer, and the noble king Pelasgus was probably slain. The women were forcibly married. On their wedding night, 49 of them killed their bridegrooms. One fell in love, and spared her husband.

Concluding Comment

The refugee maidens who supplicate the protection of the king of Argos stand within a sacred precinct and near its altar. This guards them from harm, a sanctuary. Such a sanctuary figured in Greek religious life as well as in Greek drama.

One might recall, while reading *The Suppliant Maidens*, that Aeschylus' poetic drama was part of an elaborate religious ceremonial. His tragedy was performed at the Great Dionysia festival in the Theatre of Dionysus, itself a religious site. And the altar located in the *orchestra* (a Greek word referring to an area in front of the spectators) was a genuine religious altar. Dramatists might utilize this altar in their plays, and we must assume that Aeschylus did utilize it when presenting *The Suppliant Maidens*.

THE PERSIANS   472 BC

Emperor Xerxes returns to the Persian
Court after the shocking disaster
at Salamis.

"Your sorrowful voice, touching my aggrieved
memory, awakens thoughts of my brave
friends lost, and my torn heart returns
the mournful strain in unwanted harmony."

Alternate title: Latin, *Persae*

DRAMATIS PERSONAE

Atossa, queen mother of Persia, widow of King Darius,
        mother of King Xerxes
Messenger
Ghost of Darius, deceased king of Persia
Xerxes, king of Persia
Chorus of Persian Elders, who compose the Persian Council
                of State

The Persians

We see another example of Aeschylus' innovative talent in this play about the Greek victory in the battle of Salamis. Many authors, even a creative one, would have dramatized a patriotic theme by focusing on Greek preparation and the Greek military as it faced and overcame heavy odds. Aeschylus did something quite different, locating the action in the Court of Persia and having the Persians comment on their decimation. A messenger informs Queen Atossa (widow of Emperor Darius, mother of Emperor Xerxes) of the proceedings at Salamis. Xerxes, enthroned on a hill overlooking the sea, witnesses Athenian naval stratagems and the crushing defeat. Xerxes also sits, symbolically, on a hill of excessive pride (*hubris*), which accounts fundamentally for the Persian disaster.

Aeschylus, who himself fought in that battle, never disparages the Persians or directly vaunts the Athenians. He disparages *hubris* and inferentially honors a people willing to risk everything to defend their homeland. He praises wisdom and caution in foreign affairs by revering the great conqueror Darius, raising by incantation the Ghost of Darius from its tomb to warn against a repeated invasion of Greece. (It was Darius who, 10 years earlier, had launched the army which met its fate at Marathon.)

This quality of sparing individuals characterizes the seven plays left to us from Aeschylus. He criticizes systems (despotism, vendetta, war, subjection of women). He criticizes human traits (*hubris*, cruelty, naked force, blind obedience to Authority). But the author always understands and sympathizes with individual people, singling out the causes which impel them in certain directions.

Only one thing Aeschylus cannot abide, and that is Tyranny. He is a Democrat through and through, and tyrants are to be defied and fought. With pen and sword, the life of Aeschylus exemplifies this philosophy.

Concluding Comment

(1) Choregos

A wealthy person was designated by the state to meet the substantial expenses of presenting the dramatic tetralogy at the august religious festivals (The Great– or City–Dionysia, the Lenaea, Panathenaea, and Thargelia). A form of public service (*liturgy*) if also an income tax, the responsibility was an honor. The *choregos*, as he was called, also entertained the poet and chorus after the performance.

The *choregos* for Aeschylus' *Persians* was Pericles.

(2) Themistocles

Unheralded in *The Persians*, in accordance with the understated patriotism of Aeschylus' plot, was the dominant hero of the Athenian defense at Salamis – Themistocles. One of the truly splendid statesmen of Classical Athens, he was in grave political trouble at the time Aeschylus wrote his play nearly a decade after the battle of Salamis. In fact, he would soon be ostracized, banished by the formidable vagaries of the volatile Athenian democracy. Some believe that the Father of Tragedy composed *The Persians* when he did in an attempt to remind people what Themistocles had done for his country.

Thucydides in *The History of the Peloponnesian War* and, later, Plutarch in his "Life" of Themistocles describe the man's cardinal accomplishments. These include his indispensable efforts before 480 BC to turn the Athenians in the direction of sea-power, maintaining that their future was at sea, that building and skillfully manning ships would lay the foundation of future safety and greatness.

Themistocles was a master politician, both in the Assembly and behind-the-scenes. He cajoled and pressured and finally convinced a majority in order to gain support for his policies and see that they were implemented properly. Themistocles had the long walls constructed which protected Athens from attack, scheming and conniving to achieve this despite Spartan opposition at a time when Sparta could have stopped them. In pursuit of his naval policy for military and commercial purposes, Themistocles created and developed the somewhat distant harbor at Piraeus, then constructed the long walls which connected Piraeus to Athens.

When Emperor Xerxes led the Persian attack on Greece in 480 BC, with Athens as his principal target, it was Themistocles who united a Hellas of contending, warring city-states. Plutarch writes,

> The greatest of all his achievements, however, was to put an end to the fighting within Greece, to reconcile the various cities with one another and persuade them to lay aside their differences due to the war with Persia.

When the Persians finally killed the 300 heroic Spartans at Thermopylae and poured through the pass heading for Athens, it was Themistocles who insisted on the astounding measure of abandoning the fortified city of Athens, placing the army on ships, sailing to the island of Salamis, and luring the Persian fleet into the straits. It was Themistocles who also sent out fake intelligence to Xerxes so that he would fight the Athenians where the latter wanted to fight.

The Persians

The abandonment of Athens takes one's breath away. (The Persians would sack the city and destroy the temples on the Acropolis.) Plutarch describes the evacuation:

> The entire city of Athens thus put out to sea. It was a sight which filled some with pity, while others were amazed at the hardihood of what they were doing. Indeed they sent off their families in one direction and themselves crossed over to the island of Salamis where they would face the enemy, unmoved by the tears and embraces of their loved ones.
>
> Pathetic were the old men, who were left behind because of their years, not to mention the domestic animals, who displayed a heart-rending affection and ran along howling piteously by the side of their masters as they went on board ship.
>
> The story has been recited of the dog which belonged to Xanthippus, Pericles' father. It could not bear to be separated from him, leaped into the sea, swam across the strait alongside its master's warship, and dragged itself onto Salamis island, where it fainted and died on the spot. Its tomb, they say, is the place named simply the Dog's Grave, a place pointed out to this very day.

SEVEN AGAINST THEBES   467 BC

The Spy. Eteocles, high king of Cadmus' folk,
I stand here with news certified and sure
From Argos' camp, things by myself descried.
Seven warriors yonder, doughty chiefs of might,
Into the crimsoned concave of a shield
Have shed a bull's blood, and, with hands immersed
Into the gore of sacrifice, have sworn
By Ares, god of war, and by thy name,
Blood-lapping Terror, *Let our oath be heard –*
Either to raze the walls, make void the hold
Of Cadmus – strive his children as they may –
Or, dying here, to make the foemen's land
With blood impasted.

DRAMATIS PERSONAE

Eteocles, king of Thebes, son of Oedipus
Messenger
Antigone and Ismene, sisters of Eteocles and Polyneices,
                          daughters of Oedipus
Herald
Chorus of Theban Women

Seven Against Thebes

This concerns the civil war between the sons of King Oedipus. After the blinded Oedipus had abdicated the throne and gone into exile, his brother-in-law Creon became regent for the two young princes, Eteocles and Polyneices. Upon coming of age, they were crowned joint rulers of Thebes.

The arrangement stipulated that one king would rule for a year, the other one ruling the next year, alternately. The ambitious Eteocles occupied the throne in the first year and drove his brother into exile. There, Polyneices enlisted the aid of other states, assembled an army composed of seven contingents, and assaulted Thebes to wrest the kingdom away from the usurper.

Aeschylus' drama features the pressured yet self-confident young Eteocles as he strives to shore up the city's defenses against powerful forces menacing the gates, and the Chorus of Theban Maidens who will be prime victims should the invaders succeed. We grasp an idea of the psychology of city-dwellers when the walls are assailed by a hostile army, the realistic fears of the helpless should the enemy breach the defenses and prevail.

At the conclusion, Eteocles and Polyneices kill one another in single combat. Aeschylus, himself a seasoned warrior, depicts the tremendous crisis of a city under siege, denouncing war and especially civil war. Again he underscores the adage, "Man learns wisdom from suffering", with metaphoric imagery telling us that Ambition for territorial dominance results in the acquisition of just enough ground in which to be buried.

Concluding Comment

The theme of hostility and combat between Eteocles and Polyneices, offspring of the unwittingly incestuous union between Oedipus and his mother Iocasta, must have been frequently alluded to in Greek Drama and often enough portrayed in some aspect. It would have provided a piquant topic highly symbolic of civil strife and warfare, such internecine conflict posing an everyday prospect of reality among and within the ancient city-states of Greece.

We have no idea how many renditions of the theme failed to survive. How many authors, their very names unknown to us, composed upon the theme?

Nevertheless, each of our three commemorated tragic poets have left us an adaptation of this clash between brothers. One may, with some interest, compare the treatments by the three distinctive dramatists.

Aeschylus in *Seven Against Thebes* concentrates on the psychological state of city-dwellers when under military threat, and also on the nature of leadership. In our Sophocles-chapter, one will observe how that tragedian focused on the moral dilemma faced by the sisters of Eteocles and Polyneices after the brothers have slain one another (*Antigone*). Euripides, in his *Phoenecian Maidens*, approximates the plot of *Seven Against Thebes*. However, he takes a wholly different stance on the question of leadership, and lets ironic humor send a message which Aeschylus recited with majestic force.

PROMETHEUS BOUND   c. 460 BC

Hermes. I speak to **you,** clever scoundrel, bitterness
incarnate, sinner against the gods who
gave away such honors to lowly,
short-lived human beings, you thief of fire.
The Father [Zeus] orders you to disclose what
danger menaces him, by what means he will
be overthrown.

Mark me, no riddles, only the plain truth,
each point enunciated precisely.

Prometheus. Your insolence suits your position as
an underling of the gods.

Hermes. Again we hear that proud stubbornness which
sailed you into the harbor of despair.

Prometheus. Make no mistake, I would not exchange
my hard lot for your servitude.

Hermes. Oh, better to be a servant of this rock, is it,
than the trusted messenger of Zeus!

DRAMATIS PERSONAE

Force and Violence, henchmen of Zeus, king of the gods
Hephaestus, the divine smith and craftsman
Prometheus, the rebellious titan
Oceanus
Io, the unjustly afflicted and wandering maiden
Hermes, messenger of the gods
Chorus of the Daughters of Oceanus

Prometheus Bound

This famous play inspired Goethe's and Shelley's idealism, each writing a poem about Aeschylus' titanic symbol of Freedom, Justice, Compassion, and courageous defiance of Tyranny. Aeschylus created an ethical archetype for all time.

Dramatis Personae

Prometheus. The magnificent Titan, his name means "forethinker" as he has the gift of prophecy and sage counsel. He sided with Zeus and the Olympian gods in their battle against the old order of titans, the gods winning out, thanks largely to Prometheus' guidance.

Zeus wanted to destroy the lowly human race, but Prometheus' compassion rescued human beings. He stole fire and gave it to the despised denizens of earth, allowing them to gain intelligence and all the arts. Zeus, a tyrant whose agents are Kratos (Force) and Bia (Violence), has Prometheus chained to a cliff in the middle of a deep gorge in farthest, desolate Scythia.

The antagonism between Prometheus and the Tyrant clearly reflects Greek history, and the author's political principles. From what we can glean of the missing parts of the **Prometheia** trilogy, Aeschylus again dramatizes the adage, "Man learns wisdom from suffering."

Hephaestus. The divine smith has been given the task of chaining Prometheus to the mountainside. His is a sympathetic figure surrounded by Force and Violence. The fact that the hero stole fire from Hephaestus' forge makes the smith a laudable persona indeed.

Chorus of Oceanides. The ocean nymphs possess wisdom and feeling, sympathizing with Prometheus while advising him to be practical and capitulate to authority. Yet they too become uncompromising and self-sacrificing when Zeus' despotism in the form of Hermes alienates them. (What a fine chorus this is.)

Oceanus. Another compassionate though pragmatic figure, the personification of the great ocean visits Prometheus to offer assistance. The rather simple fellow provides a faint touch of humor in a tragedy otherwise deadly serious.

Io. The cow-maiden has been compelled to suffer unimaginably, involving the same source that tortures Prometheus. Zeus, the king of the gods, lusted after her. Queen Hera, out of jealousy, afflicted the innocent girl with physical aspects of a cow. As such, a gadfly follows and stings her incessantly. Homeless, she wanders the earth in this terrible way. As Prometheus symbolizes mankind suffering under unjust government, so Io betokens both this and Woman's particular oppression by male-dominated social forces.

Io visits Prometheus, and asks the prophet when her suffering will end. Despite their own sorrows, each truly commiserates with the other.

Hermes. The messenger of Zeus is harsh and threatening. Aeschylus brushstrokes this willing lackey of despotic coercion into real life.

Each of Prometheus' encounters adds its own enhancing elements to the theme of brutality versus compassion, and to the basic plot of one great ethical hero standing up against overwhelming, tyrannical force.

Observe the crucial fact that Fate stands above the gods, and the oracle Prometheus knows that Zeus will be overthrown and by whom. He must endure suffering, for a thousand years if necessary, and not reveal the secret.

Prometheus' and Io's fate are intertwined. He tells the maiden that she must bear her painful existence for a dozen generations. Then a descendant of Io will give birth to a son by Zeus himself. This will change everything.

Hermes comes to frighten the secret out of Prometheus, but must leave empty-handed after a sharp exchange. His threats are not empty, however, and the play closes with earthquake and thunder, in the midst of which Prometheus and The Daughters of Oceanus sink into an abyss. The hero will be restored eventually to the surface of the earth – to be repeatedly attacked by a ravenous eagle which will tear at his liver, an endless torture.

Postscript: From scattered evidence, we know of a *Prometheus Unbound (Lyomenos)* by Aeschylus to follow *Prometheus Bound*. We know too that Io's descendant, the son of Zeus spoken of in the prophecy, will come to that barren cliff. It is Hercules. As the bird of prey swoops again to attack Prometheus, Hercules fits an arrow to his bow, prays to Apollo to guide the shaft, looses it and kills the predator. Hercules then wrenches away the chains, and sets Prometheus free.

Concluding Comment

The titan Prometheus has moral power, an astonishing endurance, and symbolic power. He is a giant in physical size, superhuman by nature, suffused with passion, defiant even to the King of the Gods. He is the benefactor and savior of mankind, doing what no one else dreamt of doing.

In every way, this hero created by Aeschylus looms large and vital – a hero of heroes.

Yet, imagine, the rebellious titan Prometheus, for the length of this moving, spirited, agonizing drama, **never moves.** Chained to a cliff, Prometheus throughout the play is a stationary figure. He cannot move. Inactive and still as a physical entity, he paradoxically presents as dynamic a mighty protagonist as life and literature provide us.

The *ORESTEIA* Trilogy   458 BC
(Agamemnon, Choephori, Eumenides)

This is one of the monumental works in the history of Literature. In the "Tragedy" section of the *Encyclopaedia Britannica*, it was written that,

> Even in the 20th century,
> the ***Oresteia*** has been acclaimed
> as the greatest spiritual work of man.

AGAMEMNON

The palace Watchman
has the opening speech.
"I pray to the gods in heaven to relieve me
of this service, to put an end to this watch
which has lasted one long year.

"I lie here, uneasily, like a watchdog, upon
the roof of the palace of the house of Atreus,
and have become all-too familiar with
the concourse of stars in night's firmament.
How well I know the splendors of the heavens,
those regal lights, their rising and setting,
and the seasons whether of heat or cold.

"In place of soothing sleep, I sometimes treat
my spirit with music, to sing or to whistle,
but soon my tears emerge, bewailing the
misfortune which haunts this house,
unguarded by honor as in bygone days."

DRAMATIS PERSONAE

Watchman of the palace
Clytemnestra, queen of Argos, wife of King Agamemnon
Herald
Agamemnon, king of Argos
Cassandra, captured daughter of the deceased King Priam
of Troy, concubine-slave of Agamemnon
Aegisthus, paramour of Clytemnestra, cousin of Agamemnon
Chorus of Argive Elders

Agamemnon

King Agamemnon, proud and ambitious commander-in-chief of the Greek forces at Troy, returns in triumph to Argos after ten years. He brings with him the clairvoyant Trojan princess Cassandra, his concubine.

Awaiting him is the Queen, Clytemnestra, sister to Helen of Troy. During his absence she has taken a lover, Agamemnon's cousin Aegisthus. She has ruled Argos for these ten years.

Aside from references in the text, mere mention of the names Agamemnon, Clytemnestra, and Aegisthus yields important information to a Greek audience, conjuring up the curse on the House of Atreus. Aegisthus' father Thyestes seduced the wife of his brother Atreus, father of Agamemnon and Menelaus. Atreus avenged himself by killing the seductor's sons (only Aegisthus remained alive) and serving them up to Thyestes as part of a banquet. Aegisthus is determined to kill his uncle's son, Agamemnon.

Before attacking Troy, the 'thousand ships' of Greece gathered at Aulis harbor. No winds blow, and the seer Calchas pronounced that Agamemnon's eldest daughter Iphigenia must be sacrificed to loose the ships. The King sent for his daughter, pretending that she was to marry the hero Achilles. Iphigenia arrived in Aulis, was ritually slain, and Agamemnon went on to Troy and military glory.

Aeschylus' Queen Clytemnestra is intelligent, forceful, brave and daring. A tigress. She hates her husband for that terrible deed, resolves to kill him, and plans to use her wiles to mete out justice personally.

Agamemnon arrives in a chariot with Cassandra and entourage. Clytemnestra entices him to tread upon a purple carpet of silk leading from the chariot to the palace. This symbolizes his *hubris*, overweening pride which may bestir divine anger. During the ritual bath customarily given a returning warrior by his wife, Clytemnestra enforces her symbolic victory with cold steel.

The first part of the *Oresteia* trilogy ends with the Queen standing calmly over the bodies of Agamemnon and Cassandra, Aegisthus speaking of his revenge and threatening the Chorus of Elders, then Clytemnestra stopping him from violent action. She proclaims the hope that there will be no more bloodshed, and that they may rule in peace.

HIGHLIGHTS of this majestic tragedy at the dawn of the genre include the Watchman's eerie soliloquy to open the play, the old Watchman being loyal to King Agamemnon but fearing the Queen; Clytemnestra's very presence which inspires awe, and her luring of Agamemnon onto the purple carpet of *hubris,* whose color also signifies the blood of Iphigenia; the allegory of the lion-cub; the Chorus' biblical addresses on Virtue and Reward, Sin and Retribution; Cassandra's premonition of death and her vision of the giant robe in which Clytemnestra ensnares the King and requites him; the confrontation between Chorus and Queen as she emerges from the murder-room; and Aegisthus' triumphant speech which describes the Thyestean banquet of his father and brothers.

Agamemnon

Concluding Comment

We witness one example of "the moral grandeur of the ancient world" in Aeschylus' opening play of the *Oresteia* trilogy. He made a striking ethical transformation of Homeric conceptions of the Agamemnon-Clytemnestra-Orestes tragic figures.

In Homer (the *Odyssey*), Clytemnestra's slaying of her husband was represented in the darkest terms. Agamemnon stood near Achilles and Ajax in military prowess, a badge of honor. Clytemnestra was blackened as a contemptible murderess, killing the heroic commander-in-chief without a semblance of moral justification. Orestes, in his turn, willingly took up the duty of vengeance. He slew his mother without hesitation or remorse, and was blessed by the epic poet as a filial, righteous son.

Aeschylus alters all this, attacking the blood vendetta aspect of the heroic code by changing the philosophical view of the protagonists. Agamemnon's military rank and feats of valor shrink toward insignificance when compared to the overweening ambition which led him to the ritual sacrifice of his own daughter. The author draws Clytemnestra with heroic lines, placing her as the instrument of divine justice. Orestes does not appear in the trilogy's initial drama, but he is a central figure in the following plays. You will see that Aeschylus' portrait of Orestes differs markedly from that of Homer -- a psychological world of difference.

"The greatest achievement of the human mind", the poet Swinburne denominated the *Oresteia*. A magnificent, morally idealistic achievement certainly, and the *Agamemnon* takes a giant dramatic stride toward that accomplishment.

THE CHOEPHORI
(The Libation-Bearers)

Orestes opens the play, standing
by the tomb of Agamemnon near the
palace in Argos. He is alone.

"Lord of the shades and patron of the realm
That erst my father swayed, list now my prayer,
Hermes, and save me with thine aiding arm,
Me who from banishment returning stand
On this my country. Lo, my foot is set
On this grave-mound, and herald-like, as thou,
Once and again, I bid my father hear.
And these twin locks, from my head shorn, I bring,
And one to Inachus the river-god,
My young life's nurturer, I dedicate,
And one in sign of mourning unfulfilled
I lay, though late, on this my father's grave.
O my father, not beside thy corpse
Stood I to wail thy death, nor was my hand
Stretched out to bear thee forth to burial."

DRAMATIS PERSONAE

Orestes, son of Agamemnon and Clytemnestra
Pylades, inseparable friend of Orestes
Electra, sister of Orestes, daughter of Agamemnon and
        Clytemnestra
Woman-Doorkeeper
Clytemnestra, queen of Argos
Nurse, of Orestes when he was a child
Aegisthus, paramour of Clytemnestra
Chorus of Slave Women

The Choephori

The second part of the trilogy begins with Orestes, son of Agamemnon and Clytemnestra, standing by the simple "unhallowed" tomb of Agamemnon. Commanded by the god Apollo, the young prince -- exiled as a child by his mother -- has returned to avenge his father.

His sister, Electra, enters with attendants to pour ritual libations at the tomb. Electra reveres her father's memory, detests her mother and the paramour Aegisthus who have virtually enslaved her, and lives only for her brother Orestes one day to return and wreak vengeance.

Much of the play after the brother-sister recognition scene involves Orestes' working himself up -- overcoming his abhorrence -- to kill his mother. Electra and the Chorus of Serving-Women give him forcible support, indeed pressure him. They pray to the spirit of Agamemnon for Orestes to gain will and capacity for revenge. (Awakening the Ghost of Agamemnon to take possession of Orestes represents Orestes' passions subduing his natural reluctance to murder his own mother.)

Orestes emphasizes the reasons he has for going through with it. His desired determination momentarily fails when he thinks of the Furies and their blood retribution for kindred blood spilled. At the end of this *tour de force* Invocation-scene, Orestes finally resolves. With the help of cousin and close friend Pylades, he commits matricide. Aegisthus also falls.

Thus, Clytemnestra acted as Fury to Agamemnon because of Iphigenia's blood, and because of the Curse on the House of Atreus. Orestes acted as Fury to Clytemnestra and Aegisthus because of Agamemnon's blood, and because of the Curse.

In the last verses of the *Choephori*, when the Chorus congratulates the matricide on revenge well taken, Orestes looks around to see what the Chorus cannot see -- the black hags of Nemesis, the Furies. Now, because of Clytemnestra's blood, it is Orestes' turn.

Concluding Comment

Chorus. Nothing shall be hidden from you.
   Your father, King Agamemnon,
   his hands and feet were lopped from
   his body by the same hands that buried
   him without ceremony.

Orestes writhes at the thought that his father's corpse was dismembered by his mother. The gruesome mutilation spurs Orestes to revenge.

The intention underlying the mutilation was to prevent the ghost of the slain from chasing the killer. Aeschylus wishes the audience to associate the primitive conception and barbaric practice with the system of blood vendetta against which he posits a civilized, compassionate jurisprudence.

THE EUMENIDES

The temple of Apollo at Delphi.
Orestes clings in terror to the
central altar, surrounded by the
sleeping Furies. Apollo appears
and addresses the youth he himself
had ordered to slay his own mother.

"I will never abandon you. I am your protector,
whether close by your side as now, or when
great distances separate us. I guard you and am
unalterably opposed to your enemies until the
conclusion of this matter.

"These accursed fiends, see how they now
sleep under my spell. Subdued are these ancient
hags whose womanhood neither god nor man nor
beast can ever approach. They were created for
the sake of evil, and dwell in the dark abyss of
Tartarus beneath the earth, these demons hated
by both men of the earth and the gods of
Olympus.

"You must flee with all speed and never lose
heart, for they will hunt you wherever you roam
on land or sail over the sea or tread on the island
homes of mankind."

DRAMATIS PERSONAE

Priestess of Apollo
The God Apollo
Orestes
Ghost of Clytemnestra
The Goddess Athena
Attendants of Athena
Jurors of the Areopagus, 12 Athenian Citizens
Chorus of Furies

The Eumenides

The final play of the trilogy commences at Apollo's temple in Delphi. Orestes has fled there, pursued by the Furies (who signify, besides punishment for crime, Orestes' own pangs of conscience). A horrified priestess glimpses a bloody Orestes clinging to the altar for protection, surrounded by sleeping Furies. The Ghost of Clytemnestra enters to rouse them to vengeance. Apollo arrives to chastise the Furies and declare Orestes' absolution for the matricide. Apollo delivers here one of the most vividly terrifying speeches you have ever read. Only the allegorical story in the *Agamemnon* of a domesticated lion cub -- symbolizing Helen of Troy -- growing up to kill everyone in the family, will chill your blood more arctically.

Orestes flees to Athens on Apollo's orders, the merciless Furies giving chase. Their chant-and-dance of Death highlights the drama.

Orestes, Apollo, and the Furies become participants in a trial at the Areopagus court in Athens, Orestes charged with matricide. The goddess Athena presides over a mortal jury of twelve Athenian citizens. Majority vote spells guilt or innocence. The Furies (or Erinyes) act as the prosecution; Apollo defends. Argumentation concluded, the jury divides six and six. Athena casts the deciding ballot -- for acquittal.

The Furies in their anger threaten to lay waste the land. Athena offers them home and homage in Athens, respect for the principle of punishment for crime -- but under **law** -- and names them Eumenides, the Benevolent Ones. The Furies accept the compromise, and the trilogy ends in reconciliation and celebration among both gods and men.

Concluding Comment

The Furies are hideous in appearance and terrifying in their relentless pursuit of a victim. They are indeed hellish spirits, ascending from Hell in order to kill.

However, make no mistake, they are not evil. The Furies have a job to perform, as they are executioners. They believe in the worthiness of their task -- an eye for an eye being their credo. That principle belongs to the value system of blood vendetta against which the *Oresteia* contends.

Demonic though they were, tormenting and destroying, these Erinyes were often an answer to a prayer. The prayers came from people demanding that justice be meted out to a murderer or other malefactor. The Furies were awakened by the cries of the injured. They awakened, arose from the depths, and set off on their deadly mission.

In the opening scene of the *Eumenides*, a scene of "sleeping justice" unfolds. The Furies surround Orestes, but they sleep, Apollo having induced their slumber with his divine power. The Ghost of Clytemnestra cries out for them to regain consciousness and slay her murderous son, demanding retribution.

Here is the idea as portrayed in Homer's epic, the *Iliad*:

> Meleagros lay with anger festering within him,
> his mother's curses stirring the cauldron of his
> fury, the curses which she hailed upon him
> because of the death of her mother.

The Eumenides

She, lying prostrate on the ground, tears
Streaming, prayed to Hades, and the goddess
Persephone to kill her son.
And Erinys, the mist-walking, She of the heart
without pity, heard her out of the dark places."

IX.571

Commentary on the *Oresteia*

What has Aeschylus actually shown in the *Oresteia*, in addition to the compelling story of murder and revenge, conscience and torment, gods and goblins? The Father of Tragedy has rendered a symbolic account of the primitive system of family vendetta to redress grievance, the endless process of blood begetting blood, of the hunter becoming the hunted.

To tell the tale which represented a genuinely harsh reality, Aeschylus created an atmosphere of fear tantamount to nightmare. Imagery of darkness and of blood pervade the trilogy. The moral scheme he describes was one of sin leading to retribution, on and on. In the case of King Agamemnon, pride and ambition -- *hubris* -- come before a fall.

This primitive system of blood vendetta has given way in democratic Athens to one of impartial governmental law, jury trial, and adversary proceedings aiming at justice with compassion. The bloodletting stops with one alleged crime and, were the accused adjudged guilty, one punishment.

Symbolism extends to the political sphere. Democracy, especially in Athens, is the home of equity and peace. To Despotism and Anarchy belong arbitrary bloodshed and violent factional or kinship strife.

Reconciliation, harmony, and festivity among divinities, among mortals, and between gods and men -- as seen in the finale -- speaks of peace and a bright future in Athens and among the city-states of Greece. Athens stands as a model of democracy and jurisprudence, peace and justice -- for all the world to emulate.

Aeschylus thus furnishes divine ordinance and sanction for the evolution of Justice. A moral purpose -- divine Justice or benevolent Fate -- operates in history.

The now famous Aeschylean proverb of redemption, which assumes a variety of forms in the *Oresteia*, describes the often painful human condition together with an optimistic assurance for the future of our race:

Man learns Wisdom from Suffering.

Appendix to the *Oresteia* trilogy

Here is the Lion-cub story from the *Agamemnon*, an example of the powerful verse of Aeschylus. The animal pet signifies the cause of the Trojan War, Helen of Troy.

> There was a shepherd once who reared at home
> A lion's cub. It shared with suckling lambs
> Their milk -- gentle, while bone and blood
>   were young.
> The children loved it; the old watched and
>   smiled.
> Often the shepherd held it like a child
> High in his arms; and often it would seek
> His hand with soft eyes and caressing tongue,
> Tense with the force of hunger.
>
> But in time
> It showed the nature of its kind.
> Repaying its debt for food and shelter,
> It prepared a feast unbidden.
> Soon the nauseous reek of torn flesh filled
>   the house.
> A bloody slime drenched all the ground
>   from that unholy slaying
> While helpless weeping servants stood and
>   stared.
> The whelp once reared with lambs, now
>   grown a beast,
> Fulfills its nature as Destruction's priest.

(trans. Philip Vellacott)

Conclusion

AESCHYLUS -- For his intellectual and artistic brilliance, for his ethical idealism and also for his personal, physical bravery, I consider Aeschylus to be one of the greatest persons in the history of the human race. Our modern age should feel obliged to learn of him, his achievements, and his time.

SOPHOCLES

The Prophet of Suffering and Redemption

(496-406 BC)

The life of Sophocles nearly spanned Athens' epochal fifth century BC, during which he wrote some 120 plays. Only seven have survived, of which *Oedipus Rex* was singled out by Aristotle as the supreme example of tragedy. Although Sophocles did not write a formalized trilogy, and his plays stand as independent units, certainly he wrote *Oedipus Rex* with the previous *Antigone* in mind, then wrote *Oedipus at Colonus* shortly before his own death to complement the other two works. So we do, I would say, have a trilogy, the Theban Saga of *Oedipus Rex, Oedipus at Colonus,* and the *Antigone,* by thematic chronology. I mention the point because such a trilogy warrants candidacy for "the greatest spiritual work of man".

Even beside the standard of Aeschylus, Sophocles composed exquisite dramatic poetry. As the region of Attica (with Athens its capital) was known for producing the finest honey, so was Sophocles acclaimed as "the Attic bee". Aristotle praised the streamlined structural perfection of his drama, coherent and compact.

Sophocles was a master of tragically ironic narrative, "Sophoclean irony" having become proverbial in literary criticism. The dramatic reversals of *Oedipus Rex* create suspense, despite our prior possession of the awful secret. In *Electra,* we and all but one of the characters know what lies beneath the sheet, yet the heroine's ironic stichomythia (stacatto responses) fascinates us.

Unlike the plays of Aeschylus, Euripides and Aristophanes, the tragedies of Sophocles do not appear applicable to contemporary Athenian politics, except that they evince a marked hostility to despotic authority. Yet he portrays tyranny with a psychological insight and eye to the vulnerable man behind the power.

Sophocles' heroes and heroines are almost all intelligent people of deep feeling. They exhibit a sensitive concern for right and wrong. Whether Oedipus or Antigone, Ajax or Deianeira, Philoctetes or Electra, they experience intense suffering. In the cases of Hercules and Philoctetes, pain can also be physical. They suffer, but they eventually learn understanding and wisdom. They acquire self-knowledge, often comprehending and confessing their shortcomings and wrongdoing. The Sophoclean tragic hero achieves an ennobling spiritual growth.

They also fall from a great height, and the term "tragic flaw" may be applied to some of them. Oedipus' quick-tempered arrogance, Creon's insolence in power, and Ajax's excessive pride all exhibit the classic Greek sin of *hubris*. Hercules' passion for women causes his tortured death.

Sometimes Virtue itself results in suffering and disaster: Antigone's moral courage and Deianeira's true love. Oedipus' relentless search for truth proves an ironic element in his tragedy.

Aeschylus concerned himself with the problems of peace and justice, in communities and between countries. Sophocles did a similar thing, but within the region of the individual human heart.

A Note on Organization
of the Plays in this Chapter

(1) *Ajax* is presented first because it was probably the earliest of Sophocles' extant dramas.

(2) Then comes the Theban saga in the following sequence: *Oedipus Rex, Oedipus at Colonus, Antigone.* Although *Oedipus at Colonus* was written long after the *Antigone,* and the *Antigone* composed prior to *Oedipus Rex,* the arrangement follows the chronology of the plots so that we have **thematic** trilogy.

(3) *Electra*

(4) *The Trachiniae* and *Philoctetes* are placed side-by-side because the stories are related. The former deals with the dying of Hercules. The latter treats of the great hero's bow-and-arrows which were inherited by Philoctetes.

Ajax

AJAX   date uncertain

Menelaus. You now hear my final word: this man receives
    no burial.
Teucer. Now you listen to my answer: he shall receive
    burial, and a fitting one.
Menelaus. I recall having once met a bold, insistent
    captain who pressed his crew to set sail in
    a tempest.
Teucer. And I once met a fellow suffused with his own
    foolishness, who was scornful and gloating in the
    misfortunes of others.

DRAMATIS PERSONAE

Thé Goddess Athena
Odysseus, ally of King Agamemnon
Ajax, the great hero of the *Iliad,* enemy of Agamemnon and
    Menelaus
Tecmessa, concubine of Ajax
Messenger
Teucer, half-brother of Ajax
Menelaus, brother of Agamemnon
Agamemnon
Chorus of Salaminian Sailors

Ajax

The tragedy recounts in a fine philosophical way the disaster which overwhelmed the massive military hero of the *Iliad*, bulwark of the Greek army at Troy. Sophocles gives Ajax an inordinate, violent pride -- again the *hubris* flaw of character so often cited in Greek Drama. (Oedipus, Agamemnon, and Creon were *hubris* figures.)

According to the myth, after the death of Achilles, a contest was held to determine which hero would be awarded the weapons of Achilles. Ajax felt strongly that he had earned them, but commander-in-chief Agamemnon awarded the arms to his political ally, the resourceful and politic Odysseus.

Ajax reacts wildly. Maddened by what he deems the injustice and favoritism of the award, he wants to kill Agamemnon, his brother Menelaus (who will be accused of suborning votes), Odysseus, and anyone associated with them. Ajax leaves home sword-in-hand with murder in his heart, setting off for the Greek camp.

The goddess Athena, who seems always to be at Odysseus' side when he needs assistance, intervenes. She causes Ajax to go insane, conceiving the illusion that grazing animals in the field are actually the men he pursues. Ajax slaughters cattle, sheep, and herdsmen in a mad rampage. Returned home later, he comes to his senses and is assailed by humiliation. Typically Sophoclean, this catastrophe causes the dishonored hero to reflect upon his life, his bearing and attitudes.

Ajax becomes a true hero off the battlefield, recognizing his own faults and weaknesses. He accuses himself of overweening self-importance, of failing to understand others -- in particular Odysseus -- and of wanting to settle brutally a grievance he should not have felt. Morally redeemed, he can think only of another terrible deed to redeem himself in the eyes of the world. Despite the entreaties of his wife and friends, Ajax decides to take his own life. Which he does, walking out to the shore of the Hellespont, burying the hilt of his sword in the ground, then falling on the upraised point.

The climax of the play regards the controversy over Ajax's burial. Because of his crime, and the fact that they did not like him, Agamemnon and Menelaus forbid the hero be given honorable burial. His body must be left alone, to be despoiled by birds of the sea.

Preparations for the funeral were the responsibility of the half-brother of Ajax, Teucer, whose mother was a captive of Ajax's father Telamon. Thus Teucer lacks the social position of his brother, not to mention military prowess. However, he rises to the occasion, the truest hero of the tragedy.

Menelaus, second-in-command of the Greek forces, arrives to menace Teucer should he go through with the planned funeral -- making a death-threat. Sophocles, who has never been matched for the ethic and fire of his argumentative dialogue, creates one of the best scenes you will ever read for his finale of *Ajax*. Menelaus arrogantly attacks Teucer's parentage, vilifies Ajax, and proclaims a political theory of Hierarchy which insists upon obedience in this matter of the burial. Teucer stands his ground, lauds his brother, and enunciates a theory of Equality and Justice to defend the right of Ajax to receive honorable rites.

Menelaus departs, after casting another threat. The commander-in-chief himself, Agamemnon, enters to repeat his brother's vituperative charges. Teucer holds firm. Then Odysseus appears. Agamemnon confidently turns to his sage ally and advisor, awaiting the force of his wit and influence, backed by his sword. Odysseus, the man Ajax hated most.

Odysseus lays aside his personal enmity for the dead hero, tells Agamemnon that Ajax's military exploits must not be forgotten, and that he has earned well the full dignity of interment rites. To Agamemnon's amazement, Odysseus sides with Teucer. The king of Argos leaves, and Sophocles reserves one final sublimity for the brief exchange between Odysseus and Teucer: Teucer thanks him. Odysseus graciously offers to assist in making the arrangements for the funeral. Teucer shows appreciation for the gesture, but refuses: Ajax would not have liked that.

Sophocles once again achieves a rather profound perfection.

Concluding Comment

The question of receiving a proper burial was a very important one to the ancient Greeks. Without a funeral and its ceremonial rites, it was thought that the soul could not find peace. The soul would be condemned to restless wandering forever.

Hence the significance of burial in Greek Tragedy. Besides the *Ajax*, we encounter the prominent theme in Sophocles' *Antigone*. Euripides' *Suppliants* also treats the problem. In the *Choephori* of Aeschylus, Agamemnon had received interment, but not a hallowed one. This exacerbates the avenging anger of Electra and Orestes.

THE THEBAN SAGA

(Oedipus Rex, Oedipus at Colonus, Antigone)

OEDIPUS REX　　　date uncertain;
likely in the years
following 430 BC

Oedipus (the King).　You, contemptible thing,
who could drive a stone to anger,
will you never speak out?
Is there nothing which may affect you?

Teiresias (the blind Prophet).
You find fault with my temper,
yet do not even see to whom
you are married. Instead
you blame me.

Oedipus.　Tell me, who could remain peaceful
upon witnessing the way you disregard
our city.

Teiresias.　My silence will not stop
the future from coming.

Oedipus.　So, since the future will
inevitably arrive, you should
tell me what you know about it.

Teiresias.　I have said enough and will say
nothing further. Nurse your bitter
anger as you please.

Alternate titles:　*Oedipus the King;*　Greek,　*Oidipous Tyrannos;*　Latin, *Oedipus Tyrranus* (*Oedipus Rex* is also Latin).

DRAMATIS PERSONAE

Oedipus, king of Thebes
Priest of Zeus
Creon, brother of Iocasta, minister of Oedipus
Teiresias, the blind prophet
Iocasta, queen of Thebes, wife of Oedipus
First Messenger, a shepherd from Corinth
A Shepherd, formerly in the service of Laius, former king
    of Thebes
Second Messenger, from the palace
Chorus of Theban Elders

Silent Persons
A train of Suppliants (old men, youths, children)
The children Antigone and Ismene, daughters of Oedipus
    and Iocasta

Oedipus Rex

Aristotle judged this spellbinding, perhaps perfect play to be the highest example of the tragic genre. I am convinced that when Shakespeare composed *Hamlet*, he was purposely aiming at the level of *Oedipus Rex*.

In the tragedy, King Oedipus has a series of short and long confrontations with a variety of persons -- the hero's minister Creon, the seer Teiresias, the Chorus, a messenger, his wife the Queen, a herdsman -- as he strives to learn the identity of the former-king Laius' killer, him who defiled the land and brought the plague upon it. Momentary relief and hope accompany the gradual, inexorable revelation of the truth: Oedipus' killing of his own father and incest with his mother.

These horrifying deeds were prophesied, and Oedipus gave up his home and social position to avoid their coming to pass. Always he seeks to do right; always he seeks the truth. But his nature is passionate and proud, a sword which cuts both ways.

The many tactical turnings and ironies of the plot are circumscribed by two vital, diametrically opposed events: Oedipus rises from his courage and ingenuity in solving the riddle of the Sphinx. And he falls from his inability to escape the terrible prophecy, his inability to solve the riddle of his own parentage.

The play opens before the Royal Palace at Thebes, in the midst of a deadly pestilence. The priest of Zeus stands facing the central doors. These are thrown open. King Oedipus emerges. Priest and people all pray the King save them from the plague as he had saved them from "the hard songstress", the Sphinx.

Oedipus has a strong sense of personal worth, views himself – as do others – as a man favored by Fortune. He tells

the assembled that Creon, his minister and brother to Queen
Iocasta, has been sent to the Delphic Oracle for advice.

Creon arrives. He reports that Apollo said they must
drive out a defiling thing, banish the man who killed the
former king, Laius. Oedipus replies that he had heard of
Laius, although he had never seen him. He vows to solve
the dark mystery of Laius' death, to exact vengeance on the
murderer. He promises to find the guilty for the sake of
justice, to end the plague, and to protect himself from
potential danger. The King curses "the defiling thing" and
pledges his own unwavering pursuit.

Oedipus has sent for the blind seer Teiresias, "the
godlike prophet in whom alone of men doth live the truth".
Teiresias enters. An increasingly fierce exchange between
King and Prophet takes place which is among the most
gripping dialogue ever written.

The seer knows the truth—all of it—but cannot stand to
utter what he considers useless. Oedipus urges, then snarls.
Revealing his almost uncontrollable temper, he accuses
Teiresias of complicity in a plot to murder King Laius.
Finally, stung into reply, Teiresias says that *King Oedipus* is
the accursed defiler of the land.

Oedipus taunts the prophet with his blindness, and says
that his oracular art is blind while he has eyes only for
bribe-money. At the same time the King accuses his
minister Creon of treason. Teiresias answers that Oedipus
is the blind one, practically spelling out that the King has
killed his own father and slept with his mother. Then the
prophet leaves.

The Queen's brother returns, furious about the
accusation of treason. They argue bitterly, the Queen
coming in to make peace between her husband and her

brother. She seeks to relieve Oedipus' mind about Teiresias' statements, telling a story which, she believes, proves the fallibility of oracles.

Iocasta relates the Delphic Oracle's prediction that her former husband, King Laius, would die by the hand of his own child. The Queen gave birth to a male child and, to avoid the dreaded prophecy, the babe was tied up and abandoned to its death. Many years later, the King was murdered by robbers "at a place where three highways meet".

Far from relieving his mind, the news startles Oedipus into remembrance of things past. He asks, and his wife answers: Was Laius slain where the three highways meet? Yes. When did it happen? Shortly before you were in power over this land. What did he look like? Not greatly unlike yourself. How many armed followers did he have with him? There was a sole survivor? Where is he? When he found thee, my husband, reigning in the stead of Laius, he begged to go back to the fields to tend his flock. So I sent him.

The distraught Oedipus now tells **his** story: My father is Polybus, King of Corinth. At a banquet, a drunken man said I was not the true son of my father. What did he mean, I asked my parents. They ridiculed the remark.

But I was not completely satisfied, and to allay my anxiety I went, unknown to my father and mother, to the Oracle of Delphi to ask the ministers of Apollo what all this meant, if anything. They did not answer my question in a straightforward manner, yet told me other, terrible things; that I was fated to kill my own father and defile the bed of my mother.

I fled from Corinth to avoid the predicted doom. On my journey, a horse-drawn carriage was in my path, and the old man who was being conveyed commanded that his servants thrust me rudely from the road. This happened near the crossroads you spoke of.

The driver pushed me and I struck him, then walked past the car. As I did so, the old man slammed the two-pronged goad down on my head. My staff struck quickly, and I killed every one of them.

Having finished his story, Oedipus in misery recalls his own curse on the defiler who had slain King Laius. The Chorus calms him, however, saying he should not prejudge the facts but await the herdsman, the survivor of the fight at the crossroads. He has been sent for.

The calm, sensible advice encourages the King who inquires, Did he not speak before of **several** robbers, not one lone wayfarer? Yes, that's right. (We must note at this juncture they fear only that Oedipus killed King Laius. Horrid enough, yet all still presume that the babe of Laius and Iocasta died on the mountain upon which it was abandoned.)

This investigation continues. A messenger brings "good tidings", that Oedipus' father King Polybus has died. The Queen exclaims, "O ye oracles of the gods, where stand ye now!" The man they feared would be slain by Oedipus has died by nature, not by his son.

Oedipus asks his wife, "But surely I must fear my mother's bed?" To which Iocasta answers, "Nay. . . . Many men ere now have so fared in dreams also; but he to whom these things are as nought bears his life most easily."

The messenger happily brings further "relief": that Polybus was not Oedipus' father by blood, that the messenger himself had found the babe Oedipus on the mountain and saved him. I presented you, he explains, to King Polybus who brought you up as his own son. Not only that, but another shepherd had given the babe to him.

Who was that shepherd, the King inquires. A member, the man thought, from the household of King Laius of Thebes.

Oedipus insistently pursues the matter. Does anyone present know this Theban shepherd? The Chorus answers that it is the same man now being sought as the sole survivor of the attack at the crossroads. The Queen should know for certain.

Oedipus asks her the question. She does not answer. He pressures her. The strong-minded, intelligent Queen more than suspects the whole truth, crying out that he must stop asking questions. Just stop!

The King now thinks he understands. His mother must have been a slave, and his wife fears the humiliation of being wed to a man of low birth. He demands to know what she knows, and the Queen advises him, begs him, to give up this inquiry. But the King demands that the herdsman now be brought in. Iocasta rushes into the palace.

The herdsman arrives, and he is indeed the survivor of the crossroads attack. Frightened, he evades questioning. Oedipus persists, and the poor man seeks any way out. Oedipus stays at him, gradually increasing the pressuring menace of his interrogation. The herdsman, although cornered and desperate, will not reveal the entire truth. The King in all of his menacing majesty then gives the man one final warning, and the simple fellow breaks down. He supplies all the missing pieces to the ghastly puzzle. No question remains. The proud and great King has slain his father, wed his mother, and incestuously brought four children into the world.

Oedipus runs madly into the palace, seeking his wife and mother, and a sword. With a shout he lunges at the double doors of their chamber, breaking through them only to find the woman hanging dead from a noose. He gently takes her down. Then seeing the golden brooches on her garment, he lifts them up and drives them into his eyes again and again, cursing the sight which could not see the truth.

In the final scene, Oedipus is separated from his two young daughters. In accordance with the word of Apollo, and his own edict, "the defiler" must be banished to relieve the land of pestilence. Oedipus departs into exile.

Thus ends the tragedy of *Oedipus Rex*, Sophocles' parable of the mystery of human destiny.

Oedipus Rex

Concluding Comment

Oedipus Rex commences by informing of the terrible pestilence afflicting the land. Certainly Sophocles had in mind the plague which devastated Athens in the year 430 BC near the start of the war with Sparta. It was aggravated, or caused, by overcrowding due to the huge influx of refugees fleeing Peloponnesian invasions of Attica.

Thucydides, to my knowledge, gives history's first documentary description of the plague, a terror which would carry off countless millions through the centuries until recent times (e.g. Europe's Black Death in the Middle Ages destroyed 20 million people). It killed possibly one-fourth the population of Athens.

To quote excerpts from Thucydides' account:

> At the beginning the doctors were altogether unable to treat the disease due to their ignorance of the correct methods. In fact, the death rate among the doctors was the highest of all, since they came more frequently in contact with the sick.

> Nor did any other human art or science prove of any help at all. Equally useless were prayers made in the temples, consultation of oracles, and so forth. Eventually, people were so overcome by their sufferings that they paid no further attention to such things.

> Externally the body was not very warm to the touch. The skin was not pale, but reddish, livid,

and breaking out into small pustules and ulcers. However, internally there was a feeling of burning, so intense that people could not endure the touch even of the lightest clothing or sheets, but wanted to be totally uncovered, indeed would have liked best to plunge into cold water. Many of the sick who were not looked after actually did this, throwing themselves into the water-tanks with the purpose of relieving a thirst which was unquenchable; for it was all the same whether they drank much or little.

In addition, they were afflicted with insomnia and the desperate feeling of being unable to keep still.

The disease, which settled initially in the head, went on to affect every part of the body. If people recovered from its worst effects, it left its marks on them by seizing upon the extremities of the body. It attacked the genitals, the fingers, and toes; and many of those who survived nevertheless lost the use of these members.

And some went blind. There were also those who, after recovering, experienced a total loss of memory, not knowing who they themselves were and failing to recognize their friends.

The nature of this disease rather baffles description, such was its uniqueness. As for the suffering it caused, it seemed almost beyond the capacity of human beings to endure.

The most dreadful thing of all was the sudden

despair of the victims when they realized that they had caught the plague. They would feel a sharp sense of hopelessness, and, by succumbing in this way, lose their powers of resistance.

Then there was the demoralizing sight of people dying like sheep having caught the disease because of nursing others. This resulted in more deaths than anything else. When people were afraid to visit the sick, the infected died uncared for. In many houses all the inhabitants perished through lack of any attention.

If, on the other hand, people did visit the sick, they lost their own lives, and this was especially true of those who made it a point of honor to act properly.

Athens, on account of the plague, witnessed unprecedented lawlessness. Seeing how quick could be the changes of fortune, how the rich suddenly died and the penniless now possessed their wealth, people sought to satisfy their lusts and do so in all haste. Equally transitory seemed money and life.

As for self-denial for the sake of honor, no one showed much interest, so doubtful was survival and the enjoyment of prestige. . . . No fear of god or law or man restrained them.

As for worshipping or not worshipping the gods, what did it seem to matter when one saw the good dying indiscriminately with the bad.

As for violations of human law, no one expected to live long enough to be brought to trial and punished. Everyone felt that a far heavier sentence already hung over him, and that before its execution it was only sensible to get some pleasure out of life.

This, then, was the calamity which fell upon Athens, and the times were hard indeed, with men dying inside the city walls and the land outside being ravaged by war.

Thucydides also fell victim to the plague, but recovered.

OEDIPUS AT COLONUS
407 or 406 BC

"Fair Aigeus' son, only to gods on high
Not to grow old is given, nor yet to die.
All else is turmoiled by our master, Time.
Decay is in earth's bloom and manhood's prime,
Faith dies and Unfaith blossoms like a flower,
And who of men shall find from hour to hour,
Or in loud cities and the marts thereof,
Or silent chambers of his own heart's love,
One wind blow true for ever?"

(trans. Gilbert Murray)

DRAMATIS PERSONAE

Oedipus
Antigone and *Ismene*, daughters of Oedipus
A Man of Colonus
Theseus, king of Athens
Creon, king of Thebes
Polyneices, one of the two sons of Oedipus
A Messenger
Chorus of Elders of Colonus

Oedipus at Colonus

After the tension and passions of *Oedipus Rex* comes this melancholy, meditative poetic drama. Here the aged and blind Oedipus is a brave, noble figure of suffering and endurance, a very different hero from the great man who stepped through the portals of the Theban palace to commence *Oedipus Rex.* He has learned wisdom, and attained a goodly measure of peace alongside his beloved daughter Antigone who leads him on their wanderings.

They come to Colonus (the birthplace of Sophocles), outside Athens. Oedipus has a mission, and this place (dear to the author's heart) is his final destination. The tragedy tells of Oedipus' last day on earth.

Antigone guides her father into a sacred grove. The Chorus of Elders at Colonus, upon learning who he is, insist that he leave. Oedipus' other daughter, Ismene, arrives. She speaks of strife in Thebes, the ills of his two sons, Eteocles and Polyneices, the latter about to invade Thebes. She also informs that Creon wishes to take Oedipus back to Thebes, not with friendly intent but to keep him or his corpse near the border of the country. This will bring safety to the land, said the Delphic Oracle. Oedipus expresses his grievances against Creon and his own sons.

Theseus, king of Athens, enters. Oedipus predicts trouble between Thebes and Athens. To Theseus' wonder that conflict could spring up between the two city-states, Sophocles has Oedipus recite the beautiful and famed ode on Time and Impermanence. ("Who of men shall find from hour to hour . . . One wind blow true for ever?") The blind, abdicated king hints of the legacy of safety he will bequeath to Athens when his body shall be buried on a designated spot of Athenian land.

Theban antagonism enters with Creon whose guards seize and carry off Antigone and Ismene. Theseus forces their return.

Polyneices appears as well, seeking Oedipus' support in his war against Thebes. He departs with his father's curse upon him, a portentous act which will ultimately involve Antigone.

The sky grows dark. Thunder is heard in the distance. "This winged thunder sent from Zeus" tells Oedipus his time is near. He bids his daughters Good-bye and, led by an invisible guide (the god Hermes) walks to his final resting place. A messenger relates the mysterious, wonderful death of Oedipus. The end also bespeaks the liberation of Death from weariness and suffering, a reward for courage and endurance.

Sophocles was ninety years of age when he composed *Oedipus at Colonus*, his last play.

Concluding Comment

This haunting play was composed not long before the author's decease in very old age. It was presented at the great Dionysia festival four or five years after Sophocles' death by his grandson, Sophocles the Younger.

The circumstances surrounding the composition of *Oedipus at Colonus* involve rude, mundane matters in sharp contrast with the sublimity of the tragedy's themes and tone. Sophocles' two sons had accused him of being mentally incompetent to run his estate. They took their father to court, asking that the property be turned over to them. The tragedian's successful defense was to recite before the jury a portion of his recently completed, final drama.

Perhaps Sophocles never would have written (or finished) *Oedipus at Colonus* if not for the impetus afforded by the sordid affair. Out of the muck arises a lotus. Another Sophoclean irony, we might say.

ANTIGONE   c. 441 BC

King Creon. Thou didst indeed dare to transgress that law?
Antigone. Yes, for it was not Zeus that had published
    me that edict. Nor deemed I that thy decrees
    were of such force that a mortal could
    override the unwritten and unfailing statutes
    of heaven. For their life is not of today
    or yesterday, but from all time, and no man
    knows when they were first put forth.

DRAMATIS PERSONAE

Antigone and Ismene, daughters of Oedipus
Creon, king of Thebes
Eurydide, queen of Thebes, wife of Creon
Haemon, son of King Creon, engaged to marry Antigone
Teiresias, the blind prophet
Guard, set to watch the corpse of Polyneices
First Messenger
Second Messenger, from the palace
Chorus of Theban Elders

Antigone

In this concluding portion of the Theban Saga trilogy, Eteocles and Polyneices have slain each other during the war of the Seven against the city. Creon becomes king. He decrees that the invader Polyneices be denied the honorable burial given to his brother. Should anyone try to consecrate the corpse, the penalty is death.

Antigone calls her sister Ismene forth from the palace in order to speak in private. The unexceptional Ismene provides a background against which her bold, idealistic, combative sister stands out. Antigone reveals her determination to bury their brother, and Ismene recoils at the thought of disobeying the King's death-edict. Ismene says she has "no strength to defy the State", and will not join Antigone in such a dangerous venture. Antigone **has** such strength.

King Creon meets with the Chorus of Theban Elders, and soon a guard comes to report a serious matter to the King. The fellow is self-concerned, but droll, amazingly candid, and as kindly as his duty permits. He explains that someone had sprinkled dust on Polyneices' corpse, which astonishes the King. Creon, now that he possesses supreme power, reveals a tyrannical disposition, which ironically recalls to us Creon's reproof of Oedipus' despotic leanings.

The King's threats are not lost on the Guard who goes into considerable detail about the little he knows (implying loyal diligence), studiously absolves himself of any blame, yet finds time to backtalk the King and even psychoanalyze him. Furious at the lack of respect as much as at the violation of his decree, Creon tells the Guard he had better discover the culprit, or else. The Guard exits, leaving behind him a priceless conversation.

Unfortunately, the Guard returns, leading Antigone who has been caught. Creon questions his niece who is affianced to his son Haemon, the prince. A genuine tyrant and a male chauvinist, Creon prosecutes her. Antigone stands up to him, a splendid figure invoking divine law and human conscience against an unjust decree of government. She shares her father's courage and nobility.

The King actually condemns her to death, and he **will** kill her. The only hope enters with his son, Antigone's betrothed, Haemon. He is an admirable young man, intelligent and warm-hearted, even diplomatic. He defends the woman he loves while attempting to soothe his father's bristling temper. But even the Prince fails, and Antigone is led away to a rocky prison at a distance from the city.

The blind prophet Teiresias enters. He describes to the King the fearful failure of sacrificial rites, and the cause: the unburied body of Polyneices. Enraged, Creon blasphemously accuses him of false prophecy and of taking a bribe. Teiresias warns of what will happen to the city and to Creon's very household should the situation not be remedied. Then he exits.

The Chorus of Elders counsels the King to reconsider, recollecting Teiresias' past services to the State. A troubled Creon relents, and orders that men join him in rushing to Antigone's prison to set her free. On the way, they come across Polyneices' corpse being ravaged by dogs. Driving them off, the King has solemn burial rites performed. Finished, they hurry to the stone cell in which Antigone was imprisoned. Stones had already been ripped away, and they enter at that point.

Haemon is inside, embracing the dead body of Antigone who has hung herself. Creon approaches his son who curses him and draws a sword against his father. As Creon rushes out of the tomb, Haemon drives the sword through himself.

These events having been related to the Queen back in Thebes, she takes her own life. Creon, his life ruined, confesses his guilt. The broken man is conducted into his now silent home.

Thus ends the *Antigone*, and the Theban saga of Sophocles. This tragedy constitutes perhaps the finest depiction in Literature of the eternal, almighty human conflict between Tyranny and Conscience.

Concluding Comment

One school of interpretation, hopefully a large majority, views the heroine as idealistic, brave, righteous, and without serious blemish.

Another school interprets Antigone as guilty of *hubris*, excessive and overweening pride. This version tends to deny, or modify, her martyrdom.

The opinion held by this writer acknowledges the plausible interpretation of Antigone's character containing a **trace** of vanity or self-righteousness. I feel that Sophocles has likely given her such a trace in all of his masterfully realistic, subtle treatment of character.

But this does not by any means constitute *hubris*, whereby pride must be truly excessive and of a type to **incur divine anger and retribution**. Her element of pride, as opposed to her predominating honor and genuine devotion to a righteous cause, cannot be deemed so pronounced. And no way in heaven or on earth can I see Sophoclean gods ired by a young lady who risks and sacrifices her life for the sake of **divine law**.

ELECTRA   date uncertain

Aegisthus. Did they truly report his death?

Electra.   They certainly did. More than that,
the dead was shown to us.

Aegisthus. May I also see the body to be sure
of it?

Electra.   Indeed you may, but you shall find it
a terrible sight.

Aegisthus. You give me much joy in spite of
your intention.

Electra.   If there is joy to be gained here,
I am pleased you may have it.

DRAMATIS PERSONAE

Orestes, son of Agamemnon and Clytemnestra
Electra and Chrysothemis, sisters of Orestes
An Old Man, formerly the pedagogus (or attendant) of
             Orestes
Clytemnestra
Aegisthus
Chorus of Women of Mycenae
Pylades, a constant friend and companion of Orestes
       (in a silent role)

Electra

The Athenian dramatists adapted Greek myths. Sophocles elected to handle the story of Orestes' sister Electra in a highly unusual way, especially for him. Deep philosophical insight and moral concern, individual redemption and compassion – such elements mark Sophoclean tragedy.

But not here. Sophocles was wont to take a subject and explore moral implications, indicating a path to spiritual salvation after an intense inner struggle. The motive of Vengeance – which adhere to the Orestes and Electra characters – would not fare well with this dramatist. We would expect a very different tack.

But not here. He takes the theme of revenge, and gives his heroine the most delicious taste of it you can imagine.

Orestes kills their mother Clytemnestra, no reluctance entertained by the murderer as we find in Aeschylus' *Choephori* (or Euripides' *Electra*). Since King Aegisthus has been absent from the palace, Electra and Orestes place a sheet over the corpse of their mother and await his return. Aegisthus receives a false report that Orestes has been killed, that the feared princely avenger of King Agamemnon need no longer worry him.

Orestes and Pylades hide themselves. Aegisthus enters and gloats over the shrouded corpse, thinking Orestes lies beneath the sheet. Electra presides over the tantalizingly slow unveiling of the dead body of Aegisthus' beloved queen. Electra answers each of Aegisthus' glad and nasty statements with an ironic comment dripping with joyous poison. The stunning exchange concludes with the unveiling, after which Orestes and Pylades appear and drag Aegisthus off to his demise.

While modern critics appreciate the Sophoclean genius of irony in this play, some have difficulty believing the moral or amoral position he seems to adopt in the *Electra*. The rest of us should be content with having read another masterpiece by the peerless Sophocles.

Electra

Concluding Comment

Electra, in all versions by the three great tragic poets, has a strident, vengeful personality. She partakes of her mother Clytemnestra's force of character.

The denouement of Sophocles' drama is so riveting and impressive that one may forget a few features of the play which ought to be recollected. The beauty of the poetry, for one. And the sensitive, poignant aspect of Electra, for another.

The following speech, given to the heroine in the early going, should remind us of these features:

> "O thou pure sunlight, and thou air, earth's
> canopy, how often have ye heard strains
> of my lament, the wild blows dealt against
> this bleeding breast, when dark night falls!
> And my wretched couch in yonder house of woe
> knows well, ere now, how I keep the watches
> of the night."

THE TRACHINIAE   date uncertain
(The Agony of Hercules)

Alone with Hercules' wife Deianeira,
a messenger speaks candidly about Iole.
The kind-hearted Deianeira believes her
to be a mere slavegirl brought by her
husband to their home.

"I myself, and many other witnesses, heard this
man state that Hercules subdued Eurytus and the
proud towers of Oechalia in order to possess this
maiden. Aphrodite, goddess of love, compelled
him to such warfare. Yet now the herald shields
Love and recites a very different story."

Deianeira responds, "O, my unhappiness! What
is this danger facing me? What disturbing secret
has been disclosed to me within my own home?"

DRAMATIS PERSONAE

Hercules (Greek, Heracles)
Deianeira, wife of Hercules
Nurse
Hyllus, son of Hercules and Deianeira
Messenger
Lichas, the herald of Hercules
An Old Man
Chorus of Trachinian Maidens

The Trachiniae

This tragedy was named for the maidens of Trachis who comprise the Chorus in what might have been entitled *The Agony of Hercules*. The plot relates how Hercules' wife Deianeira sought to recapture his love with a potion that brought suffering and death instead. Sophocles gives us a brief but vivid description of the fight between Hercules and a river-god. Both were suitors for the hand of Deianeira, the victor to receive her as his bride. Hercules wins, and the happy Deianeira leaves with him for Trachis.

Fate is not kind to her, despite the fact that the mature woman we find in our play has a sterling character. Hercules lusts after other women, and he now destroys a town and its king, the father of a princess Hercules burns with lust for. He captures the princess, Iole, and sends her to his home in Trachis to become his mistress and favorite.

Deianeira recognizes the threat to her love and also to her position in the household. Yet she sympathizes with the unfortunate girl while searching for a means of winning back the heart of her husband. The heroine hits upon a solution, recalling the aftermath of Hercules' combat with the river-god.

On the way home, the bridegroom and bride were obliged to cross a river. A centaur (half-man, half-horse), Nessus, carried passengers from one end of the river to the other. Deianeira was taken first. In mid-stream, she cried out as the centaur molested her. Hercules sped a poisoned arrow into him. As Nessus was dying, he offered Deianeira a "gift" consisting of clotted blood from his wound. He said it was a love potion which she could use if her husband should ever go astray.

Deianeira now looks for the potion and applies drops of the centaur's blood to a new robe she will present to Hercules on the occasion of his military victory. She sends the gift with the herald of Hercules, Lichas, who had delivered the princess. (Lichas, by the way, had claimed falsely to know nothing of Hercules' plans for her, or even to know her identity. You will not easily forget the dialogue between Lichas and Deianeira as she pries the truth out of the double-talking agent. She had been tipped-off by a kind-hearted messenger.)

Lichas returns to Euboea where Hercules conducts a sacrificial ceremony at the seashore. The proud victor puts on the robe. Momentarily benign, the poisoned garment suddenly grips the hero in a deadly embrace. The pain sears him as he struggles to take the robe off. But all of Hercules' immense strength cannot accomplish it. The robe sticks, and the poison causes excruciating, unending pain. He is carried the long journey home.

Home, Hercules lays dying. Sophocles emphasizes the burning sensation of the poison, metaphorically resonating the burning lust for the princess which brought him to this pass. His son Hyllus, a fine young man beside himself with grief, runs to his mother and vehemently condemns her act, wrongly believing it to have been intentional. Deianeira silently retires to her room, locks the door, lies on her bridal bed, and thrusts a sword into herself.

Hearing of his mother's suicide, Hyllus realizes she could not have deliberately poisoned his father, and that he had not given her a chance to explain. The tragedy ends with Hyllus at Hercules' bedside. The dying hero orders his son to have him transported to the top of Mount Oeta, and there to set him on fire. The anguished son argues but reluctantly accedes to his father's command.

The play concludes at this point. The Greek audience would know the reason for Hercules' strange command: his soul will rise from the funeral pyre to ascend into divinity.

Concluding Comment

Hercules was worshipped as a cult-hero in ancient times thoughout the Greek world. On account of his tremendous strength, courage, and colorful Labors, one can understand his popularity and the fascination of his personality.

Hercules was also a stock character in Greek comedy, often portrayed as a gluttonous buffoon. An example of the comic hero will be found in Euripides' *Alcestis*, although – as the reader will observe – the character is laudable, lovable, and pretty terrific.

In the tragedy *Trachiniae*, however, Sophocles takes a variant look at Hercules. The dramatist first centers on his lust for women and heroic but ignoble violence in pursuit of one. Then we are focused on Hercules' agony as he dies by inches and moments.

We do not know of a sequel to the *Trachiniae*. If there were such a continuation, then the other instruction Hercules left to his son Hyllus may have real significance. That was the order to marry Iole. Perhaps therein lies an element of redemption – so Sophoclean it would be – the selfish man disclosing a benevolent wish through the oppression of his agony.

PHILOCTETES 409 BC

Odysseus addresses Neoptolemus,
the son of Achilles.

" O noble youth, worthy of your father!
When I was young and strong as you, and
proud of my courage, I had scant regard for
cleverness and tactics. Experience, however,
has given me this instruction concerning rule
and sway: The power in the arm counts for
much less than soft enchanting words."

DRAMATIS PERSONAE

Philoctetes, companion of Hercules
Odysseus
Neoptolemus, son of Achilles
Merchant, a follower of Neoptolemus in disguise
Hercules
Chorus of Sailors, companions of Odysseus and
Neoptolemus

Philoctetes

If the *Trachiniae* happens to be the first part of a trilogy, *Philoctetes* might be the third part. Hercules is dead, and the hero Philoctetes has inherited his bow and arrows ("shafts inevitable, winged with death"). In our hypothetical second part to the trilogy, at the beginning of the Trojan war Philoctetes was bitten in the foot by a poisonous snake. The terribly painful but not lethal wound cannot be cured, and the sufferer's "ill-omened cries" cannot be suffered by his comrades.

Agamemnon and Odysseus decide to abandon Philoctetes on a deserted island, which Odysseus achieves through trickery. The wounded man lives alone and unaided for many years on the island, forever in wretched pain and staying alive by dint of the bow whose deadly arrows bring him game.

Sophocles' play commences with Odysseus returning to the island. On board ship with him is Neoptolemus, son of the recently slain Achilles (by an arrow of Paris who repays Achilles for his killing of Paris' older brother, Hector, the Trojan champion). Philoctetes has hated Odysseus this long decade, and lives to avenge himself for the treachery which marooned him on the island.

The Trojan War, now in its tenth year, is a stalemate. The Greek commander learns that only Hercules' bow can bring victory. Odysseus must trick Philoctetes out of the bow, but he dares not reveal himself personally for an obvious reason. Sophocles portrays Odysseus in this drama as not only wily and resourceful—traditional attributes—but deceitful and unscrupulous. The hero of the *Odyssey* schemes to use Neoptolemus, a decent young fellow, for his purpose.

In one of the highlights of the play, Odysseus seduces the honorable Neoptolemus away from his principles with appeals to both Duty (winning the war) and Self-Interest (glory). The son of Achilles approaches Philoctetes, wins his trust, and when the archer tries to sleep through a violently painful attack of the poison, steals off with the bow and brings it to Odysseus.

In an amazing turn of events, however, before Odysseus actually has his hands on the weapon, a conscience-stricken Neoptolemus returns it to Philoctetes. The crisis involving Philoctetes' physical pain and hatred of his enemies, together with the successful conclusion to the Trojan War, is settled by a deified Hercules in a *deus ex machina* appearance.[1] He breaks the impasse by advising his friend to fulfill destiny by going to Troy. There, his suffering will come to an end, and military glory will be his. The brave endurance of suffering will bring just rewards.

---

[1] *Deus ex machina* : literally, god from the machine. Actors playing divine beings descending to earth were lowered to the stage by a crane.

Philoctetes

Concluding Comment

To my knowledge, *Philoctetes* enacts, for the first time in extant literature, a theme which *Robinson Crusoe* would make proverbial – the drama of a man marooned on a desert island. Unlike Daniel Defoe's novel, with its motifs of productive work and middle-class comforts accompanied by inner repose, Sophocles' tragedy depicts a man abandoned to profound suffering.

Philoctetes is riven with physical pain and, at the same time, tormented with hatred for the men who stranded him. His lonely, desperate existence consists of the simple cave in which he rests, and the arduous steps he takes out of it to shoot game and prolong his life.

Thinking of Philoctetes' poisoned foot-wound and hobbling gait, I cannot fail to conjure up in contrast the real-life model for Robinson Crusoe – the Scottish sailor, Alexander Selkirk. When a privateer picked him up after 4 years' isolation on the island, Selkirk was so fit he could run up and across rocky hills like the mountain goats he ran after for his sustenance.

Conclusion

SOPHOCLES – The tragic drama of Sophocles is sheer excellence. The master composed some 120 plays in his long life, and only 7 have survived. How can one possibly measure such a loss?

EURIPIDES

A great Tragedian when he wished,
more commonly a Parodist and Satirist;
As original an Artist as ever lived.

circa
(480-406 BC)

This "best-loved and best-hated" dramatist, the brilliant and original Euripides, was born around the time of the battle of Salamis. He saw Athens at its Aeschylus-Sophocles-Parthenon-Pericles-Socrates height. And he lived through all but the finish of the interminable Peloponnesian War with its accompanying blights of corruption by power and money, its demagoguery and materialistic arrogance, not to forget onslaughts of the plague. He used his literary art to combat the injustice of the moment and the doom he persistently warned against. (Athens would finally lose the war with Sparta, defeated in 404 BC.)

An effervescent intellectual, he was friends with the philosophers Anaxagoras and Protagoras. Socrates was a devotee of Euripides' plays. Like Socrates, Euripides was a tireless questioner of beliefs and moral values, and the answers he himself came up with were as unpalatable to the conventional mind as were those of the great philosopher. Euripides and Socrates could not abide the idea that "Might was right."

Stark realism mingling with unabashed fancy, subtle irony and symbolism, irresistible humor, and beautiful poetry mark the ninety plays he wrote and the nineteen which have come down to us.

Euripidean irony differs from Sophoclean. When not composing straight tragedy, the author of *Medea* and *The Bacchae* wrote parody and satire. Mock-heroic, mock-romantic, mock-pious, mock-tragic – one must be on the alert for irony, or risk utter confusion.

Euripides utilizes humorous irony to debunk myths, romantic illusions, superstition, and a variety of unhealthy notions which foster prejudice, violence, and injustice. An

120

iconoclast, he is always a humanitarian, supporting the oppressed and the disadvantaged.

He detests and satirizes bullies and hypocrites; sympathizes with women and condemns social customs and attitudes directed against them; casts children as tragic figures, without sentimentalizing. Euripides creates dignified characters from the lowest classes -- peasants, slaves, foreigners, beggars, the physically-handicapped. His poetic dramas often deal with the Trojan War and associated events (e.g. *The Trojan Women, Hecuba*). To Euripides, such a war meant brutality and blunder, death and slavery. Nothing glorious about it. Homeric heroes? The gods? What moral qualities recommend them? Assuming they ever existed.

When Euripides writes of the Trojan War, he alludes to the Peloponnesian War (431-404 BC). When he depicts heroes, he hints of the war-ethic and the warmongers who find ugliness to be honorable, glorious, and unnegotiable.

When he portrays the gods, poking with fine ironic jabs, he challenges the conceptions people commonly had of them. Gods who engage in adultery, dishonest practices, and killing were not worth emulating. And as in all times and places, it is the warmongers and oppressors of the underprivileged who invoke the gods most insistently.

Moreover, 'the gods' make money for people. The Apollo Oracle of Delphi religious organization had been pro-Persian during the fight for independence, (at least at the beginning), and it made a fortune out of divination.

Besides, and most importantly, people are responsible for their own acts. Euripides' version of Helen of Troy shows her incessantly blaming the gods for her conduct. Whether the cold, cynical Helen of *The Trojan Women*, or

121

the burlesquing primadonna of *Helen*, that lame excuse is her song-and-dance.

I will classify Euripides' extant works by my own lights, as no two critics will ever accord on this matter. Arguments still rage as to any particular drama's irony or literary sobriety. In Shakespearean terminology, Euripides wrote a number of "problem plays".

Eight are straightforward tragedies: *Medea, The Bacchae, The Trojan Women, Hecuba, Hippolytus, The Phoenecian Maidens, Electra.* That leaves *Iphigenia in Aulis,* which is not precisely straightforward, but impishly, perversely if not diabolically plotted. One stares in astonishment at Euripides' audacity. He wrote a truly gripping tragedy, marked by scalpel-incising emotional exchanges, utterly realistic. Then, in the final moments, he pulled out all the stitches!

Six are comical in the main, ranging from burlesque to parody and light satire: the satyr-play *Cyclops* (our only complete example of the genre), *Helen, Orestes, Hercules Mad, Iphigenia in Tauris,* and *Alcestis.*

Four rather defy description: non-tragic drama which contains parody or satire. I suppose we ought to call them all 'satire'. They are *The Heracleidae (The Children of Hercules), The Suppliants, Ion,* and *Andromache.*

The final play, *Rhesus,* is in a class by itself, a dark satire (in the mood and mode of Shakespeare's *Troilus and Cressida*).

Although he has been accused of being episodic, the few questionable Euripidean plots make sense in terms of symbolism, the messages he seeks to get across, and his ironic humor. Euripides wants to disillusion, to undermine attitudes and values which bolster war, social injustice, and civic conflict. It startles to see him go so far as to capsize an excellent tragedy in the finale (*Iphigenia in Aulis*), yet he had a good reason for doing it. One can only marvel at his idealism. And perhaps he just could not repress his sense of humor.

A Note on Organization
of the Plays in this Chapter

(1) *Medea, The Bacchae, Hyppolytus* are in this sequence due to the group featuring – and powerfully – a Passion versus (either) Self-Control /Reason/ Continence theme.

(2) *Rhesus, The Trojan Women, Hecuba* have Trojan War plots. *Rhesus* takes place during the War itself, *Trojan Women* and *Hecuba* involving the aftermath. Although Euripides wrote the *Hecuba* before *The Trojan Women*, thematically they ought to be reversed.

(3) *Electra*

(4) *Iphigenia in Aulis, Iphigenia in Tauris:* The former was presented in competition after the death of Euripides; yet thematically they belong in the above order. (I placed them next to the *Electra* simply on account of Iphigenia and Electra being sisters.)

(5) *The Phoenecian Maidens, The Suppliants, The Heracleidae, Hercules Mad:* The first three condemn internecine (between Greek city-states) warfare; *The Suppliants* and *The Heracleidae* focus on Athens at war with another city-state and are both pseudo-patriotic dramas; *Hercules Mad* also symbolically-ironically criticizes

Athenian warfare, its protagonist Hercules thus curiously following *The Heracleidae* (i.e. *The Children of Hercules*).

(6) *Helen, Orestes, Andromache,* and *Ion* are parodies and satires.

(7) *Alcestis* and *The Cyclops*: The *Alcestis* was presented as (or in place of) a satyr-play, a true comedy *sans* Euripides' otherwise ubiquitous anti-war, anti-aggressive-violence themes. *The Cyclops* was presented as a satyr-play, a genuine burlesque.

MEDEA 431 BC

"No home, country, or refuge to me. O, I acted unwisely the day I succumbed to that Greek's persuasion and left my father's home. Now that false husband will pay a deadly price, I swear it.

"Our children that I gave birth to, he will not see them alive. Neither will his new bride bear children for him, as my drugs will mete out to her a horrid death.

"I am not a weak, helpless woman who sits meekly, hands together, at the mercy of others. No, I am of another stamp, kindly to friends, but dangerous to my enemies. Those who live as I do gain respect and reputation."

DRAMATIS PERSONAE

Medea
Jason
The two sons of Jason and Medea
Nurse of Medea
Attendant of Medea's children
Creon, king of Corinth
Aegeus, king of Athens
Messenger
Chorus of Corinthian Women

Medea

The protagonist Medea, a barbarian princess fallen in love with Jason of the Argonauts, used her sorceress powers to rescue him and further his quest for the Golden Fleece. The sacrifices she made included killings and lifelong exile from her native land. They married and she bore two sons, settling in Corinth. A passionate woman, she married a calculating man wedded also to his ease and advancement. He will now cast her off and marry the daughter of the king of Corinth.

The tragedy focuses on Medea's fearsome plan to avenge herself upon Jason. She will accomplish it, not only by killing the princess, but by slaying their own children. Yet the mother in her rebels against the latter proposal. Medea's inner conflict between Revenge and Self-Control/Natural Sympathy is finally resolved – in favor of Vengeance. She actually murders them, the tragedy concluding with Jason shouting his grief and hatred at the sorceress who escapes through the air on a chariot drawn by dragons.

Horrid as her crime is, we sympathize with the tormented woman, and revile Jason's perfidy and hypocrisy. A powerful story, Medea warns its audience of the dangers of continued failure to respect the rights of women. Euripides also aims a blow at patriotic and racial arrogance, and at Athenian imperialism as well. The latter may even be his main point – a grim Prediction of Greek states taking their revenge on the imperial tyranny.

Concluding Comment

If ever a story dramatized the thin line separating Love and Hate, *Medea* is it. The extremes to which the heroine went as testimony to her love for Jason of the Argonauts included the murder of her own brother. The extremes to which Medea was impelled by dint of her hatred for his betrayal included the murder of her own beloved children.

If ever a story dramatized ruthless passion (Medea) opposed to "the cool brutality of civilization" (Jason), *Medea* is it. The confrontation between the heroine and her calculating lover, before the die is cast, constitutes the highlight of the tragedy. Even the inner tension and conflict of decision-making, the several murders, and the resultant anguish, pay court to this scene.

THE BACCHAE

posthumously
presented by
Euripides' son;
thus after 406 BC

Dionysus (the god of wine and revel in disguise).
You treat lightly my solemn pronouncement,
O King, paying scant attention to what
you have heard. I give you one more
warning. Do not raise a spear against a
God. Be silent and fear His anger! Should
you dare to frighten His followers away
from the hills of their delight, He will not
tolerate it.

Alternate title: *The Baccantes*

DRAMATIS PERSONAE

Dionysus, god of wine and of ecstasy
Pentheus, king of Thebes
Teiresias, the blind prophet
Cadmus, abdicated king of Thebes, grandfather of Pentheus
First Messenger
Second Messenger
Agave, mother of Pentheus
Chorus of Bacchae, the Maenads, women who worship
                    Bacchus (Dionysus)

The Bacchae

Many appraise the streamlined, gripping and wrenching tragedy to be Euripides' best play. This weird and fascinating drama, which drives on to a stunning finish, begins with a soliloquy by an incarnate god, Dionysus (Latin, Bacchus), god of wine and a symbol of Passion. He has come to Thebes where King Pentheus has forbidden his worship. (Pentheus represents narrow rationality and puritanical repression.) Dionysus has maddened the women of Thebes with his dread Mysteries, and Pentheus believes—erroneously—that the women have been seduced into loose morals.

The King does not know he deals with a God, tries to imprison Him, and becomes increasingly incensed at his adversary's inexplicable ability to thwart all efforts against Him.

An officer of the King describes the amazing dances and communion with Nature of the Bacchanal women as they wander through the countryside. When they know themselves to be watched by men, however, the women become a raging mob, each individual endowed with terrific physical strength. They attack even large animals and rip them to shreds.

Pentheus' hatred of the Stranger suddenly gives way to trust. (Passion vanquishing Judgment, the God controls the King.) Following Dionysus' lead, Pentheus goes out in the fields to watch the sacred rites forbidden to all eyes.

The Stranger miraculously pulls the top of a tall tree down to ground level, the King seats himself there, and the tree is gently straightened to its height. Pentheus has a grand view of the Bacchanal women below, but they have a clear view of him. Racing towards the King, they wrench the ash-tree out of the earth and Pentheus falls at their feet.

Among them is his own mother, Agave, with whom he
pleads for mercy. Possessed by the God, the wild-eyed
woman catches hold of her son, ripping off his arm. The
other women close in, and tear the King to pieces.

Agave carries the head of her son back home, proud of
the "lion" she has vanquished. Gradually she regains her
senses, and recognizes what she holds in her hands.

And so ends the tale; on one level at least, a parable of
Passion and Reason, that each is madness if not balanced by
the other. The Peloponnesian War, still raging after twenty-
five years (with Euripides in voluntary exile), was surely a
point of reference in this regard. Especially the Passion
which fueled three decades of bloodshed.

Whatever, the story rivets, and forces a contemplation
of inner meanings. That accords with Euripides' Socratic
style, forever spurring his audience to ponder, review, and
re-appraise values and attitudes in the direction of sober
judgment, justice and fair play.

The Bacchae

Concluding Comment

(1)   Euripides composed this sensational tragedy while in self-imposed exile.   Disillusioned with Athenian politics and continued policies of empire and war, he had wielded his ironic pen in battle for a quarter of a century to no avail. (I might mention the speculation that repressive elements in Athens were threatening him with prosecution, much as Socrates would undergo 8 years later.) When King Archilaus of Macedonia invited the famous playwright to his court, Euripides accepted. This was probably in 407 BC. He would die there, in his old age, perhaps a year later.

Before his death, Euripides wrote one of his very finest plays, this one, *The Bacchae*. The clash between universal principles in the tragedy may have summed up to him the entire tumultuous, rending epic of the Peloponnesian War.

The play was discovered after his death, and presented in Athens by his son (or nephew) Euripides. It may have been produced as part of a trilogy which included *Iphigenia in Aulis*, another great tragedy apparently composed also by the renowned poet in his foreign residence.

(2) Marcus Licinius Crassus was a Roman consul and triumvir in the second century BC. The accumulation of vast personal wealth, by whatever means, provided a dominant interest in the life of the eminently successful Crassus. He capitalized grandly on the fate of 4,000 people death-listed by Sulla in 82-81 BC. He earned plaudits and money by destroying the freedom-fighting slaves of the heroic Spartacus in 71 BC, crucifying the captured.

An ally of Julius Caesar, Crassus availed himself of Caesar's influence to obtain the choice plum of Syria. With the intent of destroying the Parthians and amassing another hill of money in addition to glory, he proceeded to the Middle East.

Crassus attacked the Parthians, and continued the onslaught at a time when the Parthian king was celebrating the marriage of his son. The festivities included a performance of Euripides' *Bacchae*, which was interrupted by a messenger who presented the King with a trophy – the head and hand of the avaricious and now-deceased Crassus. The Players adroitly appropriated the remains of Crassus to use ever-so-nicely in the climax to Euripides' drama.

HIPPOLYTUS 428 BC

Hippolytus. Mighty Zeus, how could You allow Woman to dwell under the sun, this wretched counterfeit of Man which brings him sorrow? If You had desired human beings to reproduce themselves, why didn't You devise other means than having women breed them? Wouldn't it have been better to purchase a family in Your temples? In this way we could be free and independent of these females.

DRAMATIS PERSONAE

Hippolytus,   son of Theseus by his former marriage to the
                amazon queen, Hippolyta
Phaedra, wife of Theseus
Nurse of Phaedra
Theseus
Aphrodite, goddess of love
Artemis, goddess of chastity and the hunt
Messenger
Chorus of Troezenian Women

Hippolytus

This fine tragedy adapts the myth of Hippolytus and Phaedra. Theseus, king of Athens, had been married to Hippolyta, queen of the Amazons, who gave birth to a son, Hippolytus. He grew to be an extremely handsome young man, in love with the outdoors life of hunting and coursing through Nature, devoted to the chaste goddess of the hunt, Artemis (Latin, Diana). Hippolytus himself is sexually chaste and, like Hamlet, has extreme views on women maintaining pure relations.

Theseus re-married, to the beautiful Phaedra. She falls in love with her stepson, experiencing a violent passion she tries to conceal. Phaedra is, in fact, dying from her secret, unfulfilled love. Her Nurse desperately decides to tell the continent Hippolytus of his stepmother's feelings. Theseus' absence on a journey facilitates the Nurse's endeavor.

Informed, Hippolytus explodes with anger, condemning Phaedra, her go-between, and womankind. Phaedra's shame at the revelation, and the hopelessness of her love, seals the Queen's fate. She commits suicide. But before taking her life, Phaedra leaves a letter for her husband. A poisoned missive, it accuses Hippolytus of molesting her.

King Theseus returns to find his wife dead and his son accused by her dying testament. (Euripides' irrepressible ironic humor surfaces here: Theseus has been to the Delphic Oracle—a frequent butt of the playwright's jibes. He comes back wearing a garland signifying good fortune.)

Theseus vilifies Hippolytus who denies guilt but can say nothing more since he had sworn to the Nurse not to reveal her unholy proposition. Theseus, who had been given the divine power to kill with a curse, damns his own son. As a result, while driving his chariot along the seashore into exile, Hippolytus has an accident. A huge bull materializes from a wave of the sea to charge the chariot. The horses go wild. Hippolytus falls and, entangled in the reins, is dragged towards his death. Found scarcely alive and brought home, he lingers as Theseus—who has learned the truth about Phaedra—sits with his dying son. Hippolytus consoles his grieving, repentant father.

Again, Euripides pinpoints Passion untempered by Reason as a destructive force in human affairs. Outside the theatre of drama, Socrates was drawing the same picture of life.

Concluding Comment

Hippolytus.   Great Zeus, why didst thou, to
man's sorrow put woman, evil counterfeit,
to dwell where shines the sun? [etc.]

Hippolytus may, admittedly, be a mite misogynist.
Aphrodite, the goddess of love, may have just cause to
deem him an enemy. Aristophanes, the king of burlesque
comedy, perhaps largely because of this play and the above
speech in particular, never tired of twitting Euripides for
(allegedly) portraying women in infamous fashion.

Nonetheless, the noble Hippolytus is a young man in
love. He loves, indeed worships, the virgin goddess of
chastity and hunting, Artemis. And he is in love with
nature, as exemplified by the following lovely ode.

Hippolytus.   Goddess, I have composed for you
this coronet of flowers gathered from a pristine
meadow, unswept by the farming scythe,
unsoiled by grazing flocks.
Bees thread their way in springtime over the
virgin meadow. Purity tends the garden of
flowers with waters drawn from clear running
streams. And only they whose nature is
innocent, artless, and self-controlled may be at
home there. Only they may gather the flowers.
The worldly and impure may not.
Dear Mistress, accept this coronet of blossoms
for your golden hair, a gift offered with sincere
reverence.

RHESUS   uncertain date

Hector. Assembled Trojans, listeners, Which one among you has the daring to slip through the Greek lines? Who shall offer such assistance to his country?

Dolon. I, **I** shall shall do it, O Prince! I myself offer our Troy to pass in disguise unto the Grecian ships, to overhear what they say, and report back to you.

Hector. Tell me what reward you would have – anything short of my crown.

Dolon. I do not want a royal and worry-beset life.

Hector. Do you wish to wed a King's daughter?

Dolon. I wish for no bride to look down upon me.

Hector. You can have gold, if this tempts you.

Dolon. We live at ease and care not for gold.

DRAMATIS PERSONAE

Hector, the great Trojan champion and prince of Troy
Aeneas, a Trojan leader
Dolon, a Trojan soldier
Messenger, a shepherd
Rhesus, king of Thrace
Odysseus, the resourceful and wily Greek leader
Diomedes, a Greek leader
Paris, the Trojan prince who had carried off Helen
The Goddess Athena
The Muse
The Charioteer of Rhesus
Chorus of Trojan Sentinels

Rhesus

This outstanding satire, one of the best tragic satires ever written, is possibly the earliest drama we have from Euripides. Superbly ironic, **Rhesus** interplays humorous and tragic irony in a way that perhaps only Shakespeare can match. The main character is the generous hero Hector, militarily and morally a splendid figure of a man surrounded by fools, braggarts, and assassins.

The play opens in the Trojan camp in the middle of the night with a report that the Greeks are in a commotion. This follows a great Trojan victory, and Hector jumps to the conclusion that the enemy will flee in their ships. He dons his armor to attack before they escape from the shores of Troy. Aeneas enters to chide Hector for lacking caution. Investigate first and see what the Greeks are about, he advises. Hector accepts the advice and takes off his armor.

The troops are assembled and Hector asks for a volunteer to spy upon the enemy. The brash Dolon steps forward. Dolon has the audacity to demand the horses of Achilles should his mission succeed and the Greeks routed, the renowned horses which Hector himself sought as a prize. The heroic and unselfish commander yields, and the braggart soldier starts off for the enemy lines with visions of glory and Achilles' horses in his head.

Rhesus, a braggart hero from the country of Thrace, arrives with his troops. He drives a gold-encrusted chariot and has a team of splendid white horses. We suspect "all that glisters is not gold" (a *Merchant of Venice* quote), especially after learning that Hector established him in power and that Rhesus "comes to the feast" (a quote from Hector) and conveniently late enough to avoid the worst of the war.

To our surprise, the goddess Athena—divine friend of the shrewd Odysseus—indicates that Rhesus, in fact, lives up to his big talk. If he fights for but one day, the Greeks are lost.

Odysseus and Diomedes catch Dolon who tells them everything they want to know—and with real enthusiasm— such as the password to get them through the Trojan lines. (Euripides does not give us this scene; the audience knows the event from the "Doloneia" chapter of the *Iliad.*) They kill Dolon and enter the Trojan camp looking to slay Hector asleep in his tent. Foiled here, Athena tells them of Rhesus. Diomedes kills Rhesus and his men in their sleep—they had stupidly failed to post a guard—as Odysseus steals the white horses. Then the two marauders escape, thanks to the habitual thickness of the Trojan sentries.

One man survives the onslaught, Rhesus' charioteer. He could not see in the dark, but nevertheless feels certain he knows the culprit's identity. The Trojans gather round and the charioteer loudly damns **Hector** as the killer. After all, does not everyone know how Hector values excellent horses! Thus, Hector's generosity regarding the horses of Achilles assumes a cynical symbolism: the high-minded are subject to low slander.

In the final verses, the noble Hector delivers a speech confident of victory, which rings with as finely hollow a sound as satire can muster. Euripides' typically dry-and-wry Chorus finishes the play:

146

Chorus. Obedience to our prince! Let us
   array ourselves in mail, and go forth and
   these orders tell to our allies, and haply
   the god who is on our side will grant us
   victory.

This chorus, atypically, is **un**intentionally wry, being
composed of the dull-witted sentries who let the killers in
and then out again. Only Euripides has his tongue in cheek.

Concluding Comment

Many critics have questioned or denied Euripidean authorship of *Rhesus*. Yet the dark satire is so precisely and perfectly Euripidean that one may question why anyone would have doubts. The subtle, skillful irony woven throughout the plot betokens Euripides. That we read parody as well as satirical irony confirms us in our certainty. The strong anti-war theme and the hard, negative slant on the character of Odysseus adds to the evidence. The sheer excellence of the anti-war satire decrees Euripidean authorship.

Rhesus not only **must** have been written by Euripides, but perhaps **could only** have been written by him.

THE TROJAN WOMEN   415 BC

"Men-at-arms, do your duty.
Bring Cassandra forth without delay.
Our orders are to deliver her to the
general at once. And afterwards we can
bring to the rest of the princes their
allotted captive women."

Note

   The Trojan Women and *Hecuba* will be discussed in the same essay.

Alternate title: *Troades*

The Trojan Women
DRAMATIS PERSONAE

Hecuba, queen of Troy, wife of Priam, mother of Hector
    and Paris
Andromache, widow of Hector (the deceased prince and
    champion of Troy)
Cassandra, a prophetess, daughter of Hecuba
Helen, wife of Menelaus, king of Sparta; carried off by
    Paris, prince of Troy; "Helen of Troy"
Menelaus, king of Sparta, commander of the Greek armies
    together with his brother Agamemnon
Talthybius, herald of the Greeks
Poseidon, god of the sea
Pallas Athena, goddess, special protectress of Athens and
    of Odysseus
Chorus of Captive Trojan Women

HECUBA   c. 425 BC

Odysseus. To sacrifice Polyxena, your daughter, over the grave-mound of Achilles is the will of the Greeks. They have appointed me to bring the maiden to that place for this purpose.

    Do not fight this, do not make me use force to separate you from her, do not match your strength against mine. Recognize the true situation and your limited means.

Hecuba. Do you not recall that time you came to spy upon Troy disguised in rags and foul apparel? Drops of blood fell from your cheek.

Odysseus. Recall it! Yes indeed, it made no faint impression upon my heart.

Hecuba. Did not Helen recognize you and inform me?

Odysseus. I cannot forget the terrible risk I took.

Hecuba. Did you not humbly embrace my knees?

Odysseus. Yes, I remember how my hand became cold and lifeless on the robe I grasped.

Hecuba. Being in my power, what did you say?

Odysseus. I must have found a good deal to say in order to save my life.

Hecuba. Was I not the one who saved you, letting you go?

Odysseus. You did.

Hecuba. And after this kindness shown you, are you not ashamed to act against me as you do?

Odysseus. O Hecuba, hear my words.
    Endure these sorrows.

Hecuba
DRAMATIS PERSONAE

Hecuba, queen and wife of Priam, the deceased king of Troy
Polyxena, daughter of Hecuba and Priam
Ghost of Polydore, son of Hecuba and Priam
Odysseus
Talthybius, herald of Agamemnon
Maid of Hecuba
Agamemnon
Polymestor, king of the Thracian Chersonese
Children of Polymestor, attendants, guards
Chorus of Captive Trojan Women

The Trojan Women / Hecuba

The two anti-war tragedies would preferably be read in this order. The *Trojan Women* depicts enslavement of the women of Troy by the victorious Greeks. Queen Hecuba and the great Hector's noble wife Andromache are the central victims. In vain does Andromache attempt to protect her young son Astyanax from the Greeks. They take the boy and, for raison d'etat, throw him from the battlements to his death. In contrast, a shameless Helen of Troy talks her way back into the good graces of her husband Menelaus, gliding again into the lap of luxury.

Plutarch's *Lives* (that of Pelopidas) recounts that Alexander of Phersae, a tyrant who had coldly slain many people, weeped at a performance of *The Trojan Women*.

In our *Hecuba* sequel, the aged and weary Hecuba cannot prevent her last two children from being killed. The Greeks demand her daughter Polyxena as a ritual sacrifice (to appease the Ghost of Achilles who in life had been in love with her).

In the centerpiece of the play, Hecuba entreats Odysseus to save the girl. She recalls to him how she had once saved his life when he had been caught behind the Trojan lines. Hecuba begs Odysseus to return the favor. Never putting aside his political considerations, Odysseus refuses. The brave girl is led away.

Now only one of Hecuba's children remains alive. Her son Polydore had been sent away from Troy to place him out of danger, entrusted to King Polynestor of Thrace. Hecuba, a personification of grief in classical and renaissance literature (e.g. *Hamlet*), learns that Polynestor murdered her son for the money sent along with him. The former Queen invites the King to her tent, where she and women followers blind him.

Concluding Comment

(1)   Euripides wrote his antiwar classic, **The Trojan Women**, in the wake of a horrendous occurrence – the massacre at Melos in 416 BC. The island of Melos attempted to remain neutral between Athens and Sparta. The Athenians demanded that she lend her support (they meant, in fact, subjection) to Athens or suffer merciless consequences.   This, in view of Mytilenes's near-catastrophe at the empire's hands in 427 BC (see section "Andromache") and the executed, utter destruction of Scione in 421 (see "Hecuba" concluding comment below).

Melos withstood imperial Athenian political pressure and military threat. Then the brave islanders withstood a full-scale Athenian military assault and economic blockade. They held out through the summer, the autumn, and into the winter. Then the Athenian siege, aided by treachery from within, overcame the islands' defenses. Thucydides writes, in his *History of the Peloponnesian War*, of this base chapter in the history of Athenian imperialism:

> The Melians surrendered unconditionally to the Athenians, who put to death all the men of military age whom they captured, and sold the women and children into slavery. Melos itself they annexed, sending out later 500 men as colonizers.

(V.116)

(2) The following account of the tyrant, Alexander of Phersae, comes from Plutarch's *Lives* ("Pelopidas"):

Epaminondas had learned of his cruelty and contempt for right and justice. He sometimes buried men alive; sometimes had them sewn into the skins of wild boars or bears, then set his hunting-dogs upon them, or shot them himself. Such was his amusement.

Concerning the cities of Meliboea and Scotusa, which were friendly allies, he surrounded the People's Assembly with his guards, and proceeded to slaughter them from the youths upward.

He also sanctified the spear with which he had slain his own uncle, Polyphon, bedecked the weapon with garlands, offered sacrifice to it as if it were a god, and gave it the name 'Tycho', Luck.

Once, however, when he was watching a tragedian perform Euripides' *Trojan Women*, he suddenly left the theatre. He sent back a message to the actor telling him not to lose heart or to relax his efforts because of his departure. It was not out of contempt for his acting that he had left the theatre, but due to his feeling of shame to let the citizens see him, a ruler who had never shown pity to any of the men he had murdered, shedding tears over the sufferings of Andromache and Hecuba.

(29)

Concluding Comment

Euripides composed **Hecuba** circa 425 BC (so it could have been 426). The Mytilenian Debate of 427 must have been uppermost in his mind when writing about the tragic helplessness of Hecuba in saving her children. Thucydides observed regarding the aftermath of Athens' crushing of revolt by the city of Mytilene on the island of Lesbos:

> When Salaethus and the other prisoners reach Athens, the Athenians immediately put Salaethus to death in spite of the fact that he undertook, among other things, to have the Peloponnesians withdrawn from Plataea, which was still being besieged.
> They then discussed what was to be done with the other prisoners and, in their angry mood, decided to put to death not only those now in their hands but also the entire adult male population of Mytilene, and to make slaves of the women and children.
>
> So they sent a warship to Paches to inform him of what had been decided, with orders to put the Mytilenians to death immediately.
>
> Next day, however, there was a sudden change of feeling and people began to think how cruel and how unprecedented such a decision was – to destroy not only the guilty, but the entire population of a state.

Observing this, the deputation from Mytilene which was in Athens, and the Athenians who were supporting them, approached the authorities with a view to having the question debated again. They won their point the more easily because the authorities themselves saw clearly that most of the citizens were wanting someone to give them a chance of reconsidering the matter.

So an assembly was called at once. Various opinions were expressed on both sides, and Cleon, the son of Cleaenetus, spoke again. It was he who had been responsible for passing the original motion for putting the Mytilenians to death. He was remarkable among the Athenians for the violence of his character, and at this time he exercised far the greatest influence over the people. He spoke as follows:

(III. 36)

Cleon's speech, which I recommend reading, was a first-rate example of crass, clever and sophistic demagoguery in a base cause, delivered by the foremost demagogue of the day. But Cleon did not get his way -- this time. The decree was rescinded and a swift ship sent out to overtake the other and arrive in Lesbos before the one bearing the order for the massacre. And it did arrive earlier. This time, the population was not destroyed. But Cleon, his supporters, and those who emulated him would remain powerful in public affairs. The mass murder and enslavement which almost happened to Mytilene would be executed at Scione in 421 BC and at Melos in 416.

ELECTRA   413 BC

Orestes. What shall we do?
Our mother -- murder her?

Electra. What! Has mercy seized you?

Orestes. Oh! How can I slay her?
How can I slay her who gave birth to me
and nursed me?

Electra. Kill her as she killed our father!

DRAMATIS PERSONAE

Electra, daughter of Agamemnon and Clytemnestra, sister
     of Orestes
Peasant of Mycenae, husband of Electra
Orestes
Pylades, close friend and companion of Orestes
Clytemnestra, queen of Argos, now wife to Aegisthus
Aegisthus (spoken of extensively by a messenger, though
     not appearing otherwise in the drama)
Messenger
The Dioscuri, the twin gods Castor and Polydeuces
Chorus of Argive Countrywomen

Euripides' treatment of this character and her brother differs substantially from that of Sophocles. The latter tragedian followed the traditional portrait of Orestes and Electra as single-minded avengers of their father, King Agamemnon. Euripides adopts another approach which follows the *Oresteian* lead of Aeschylus, taking up where the *Choephori* left off, adding a further reform to the Homeric avenger lauded in the *Odyssey*.

Orestes is openly torn by the Duty of vengeance on the one hand, and by Conscience's natural qualms about matricide on the other. Euripides' Electra is as determined an avenger as Aeschylus created, and seems even more so as she hounds Orestes with argument, goading him into murdering their mother. She at last succeeds in overcoming her brother's scruples, and the brother and sister together kill Clytemnestra.

The finale, however, sees both of them wracked by remorse for their deed. Euripides goes further than this to condemn the matricide. He has a god descend to tell them that, although Clytemnestra deserved her fate, her children had no right whatever to execute it.

Euripides places an even stronger emphasis on the verdict by adding bits of parodying humor: Electra's description of her part in the murder reinforces the somewhat theatrical comedy of their joint handwringing regrets. The god Castor inserts his exclamation point to this skillful caricature by stating that the all-wise prophet-god Apollo, who had ordered Orestes to commit the matricide, had simply made a mistake.

In other words, Euripides' ironic humor implies that murdering your own mother is not only wrongful. It's a bad joke.

Euripides indeed takes one long stride past this position. The murder of Aegisthus did not faze Aeschylus. Not so our *Electra* dramatist. In the real highlight of the play, Orestes murders Aegisthus in the royal garden after the King had hospitably welcomed Orestes and Pylades (in disguise). A brutal scene, it satirically conveys to the audience the unconscionability of a cold-blooded killing – whatever the motive. With this extraordinarily compelling dramatization, Euripides registers once again his deep-seated aversion to aggressive violence.

Concluding Comment

Electra contains a recognition-scene between Electra and her brother Orestes, as does Aeschylus' *Choephori*. Euripides jests about the plausibility of Aeschylus' scene whereby Electra recognizes, after many years, the locks of hair Orestes leaves on their father Agamemnon's grave. (Orestes was exiled when still a small boy.)

Aeschylus wrote:
Electra. And lo! in truth the hair exceedingly like –
Chorus. Like to what locks and whose? Instruct me that.
Electra. Like those my father's children wear.
Chorus. Then is this lock Orestes' secret gift?
Electra. Most similar it is to the curls he wore.

Euripides parodied:
Old Man. And lo!.... severed locks of auburn hair. Much I wondered, my daughter, who had dared approach the tomb; certainly 'twas no Argive. Nay, thy brother may perchance have come by stealth, and going thither have done honor to his father's wretched grave.

Look at the hair, compare it with thy own, to see if the color of these cut locks is the same; for children in whose veins runs the same father's blood have a close resemblance in many features.

Electra. Old sir, thy words are unworthy of a wise man, if thou thinkest my own brave brother would have come to this land by stealth for fear of Aegisthus. In the next place, how should our hair correspond? His is the hair of a gallant youth trained up in manly sports, mine a woman's curled and combed. Nay, that is a hopeless clue.

Besides, thou couldst find many whose hair is of the same color, albeit not sprung from the same blood. No, maybe some stranger cut off his hair in pity at his tomb, or one that came to spy this land in secret.

IPHIGENIA IN AULIS

posthumously
presented by
Euripides' son;
thus after 406 BC

Agamemnon.	Ha! What's this? What means this brawling at my very gate?
Menelaus.	Hear me! I am the one to speak, not he.
Agamemnon.	Menelaus struggling with my man? How's this?
Menelaus.	First look me in the face and then I'll speak.
Agamemnon.	You think I dare not? I, King Atreus' son?
Menelaus.	You see this tablet, you know its shameful words?
Agamemnon.	It's mine. Give it to me.
Menelaus.	No, not until I show the army what you've written there.

DRAMATIS PERSONAE

Agamemnon, commander-in-chief of the Greek armies
Menelaus, brother of Agamemnon
Clytemnestra, queen and wife of Agamemnon
Iphigenia, daughter of Agamemnon and Clytemnestra
Orestes, small son of Agamemnon and Clytemnestra
Achilles, the great martial champion of the Greeks
An Old Servant of Agamemnon
Messenger
A Second Messenger, in the Epilogue
Chorus of Women from Chalcis

Iphigenia in Aulis

The Greek ships are moored at Aulis harbor where the absence of sea-winds stops their advancing to Troy. Agamemnon is commander-in-chief of the allied Greek forces; his brother Menelaus is second in command. The flight of Menelaus' wife-and-queen Helen with Paris, a prince of Troy, has caused the war.

The seer Calchas divines that the anger of the goddess Artemis stymies the ships, and that only the ritual sacrifice of Agamemnon's daughter Iphigenia will allow them to depart.

Agamemnon loves his daughter but is highly ambitious. He writes to wife Clytemnestra back in Argos to send Iphigenia to Aulis where she will (ostensibly) be married to the hero Achilles. Later, the father regrets his decision and writes another letter countermanding the first. A faithful servant carries the letter from his tent but is intercepted by the suspicious Menelaus who wants the war prosecuted at all costs. Agamemnon enters and a sensational Quarrel-scene begins. Finally, a messenger announces that Clytemnestra and Iphigenia have arrived in Aulis. The letter has become immaterial.

Eventually, Agamemnon's wife and daughter learn of the true reason Iphigenia was sent for. They plead with him, but to no avail. Clytemnestra goes to Achilles – her only hope – to beg his help. The hero promises his assistance in strong terms. However, all that he will actually deliver are excuses, and he will participate prominently in the rites leading to the sacrifice of the maiden.

Euripides deftly satirizes Achilles' treachery. Thus the play has moved from straightforward tragedy to tragic irony, and the author concludes the play with satire and spoof. As the knife descends on Iphigenia, she is whisked away by a divine power, Artemis. The infallible seer Calchas, whose prophecy precipitated the crisis, casually states that the sacrifice was a bad idea and would probably have defiled the altar. Agamemnon expresses joy at his daughter's good fortune at being with the gods, and at his own prospects for winning "undying fame" at Troy. Clytemnestra, for her part, doubts in fact what happened, and wonders if they are not telling a fairy-tale to cheer her up.

In sum, 98% of *Iphigenia in Aulis* forms one very great tragedy. The finale most remarkably descends into comic irony. Euripides was not content to write brilliant drama illustrating acceptable moral values. He must stimulate the audience to ask questions and ponder for themselves the deeper meaning of things.

Concluding Comment

Of the 44 Greek plays which have come down to us from Classical Athens, only *Iphigenia in Aulis* casts Achilles as a character in the drama. And Euripides' characterization is superb, memorable and indelible, bitingly satirical, realistic.

The *Iliad's* independent, uncompromising, fearless and invincible martial champion becomes something else in Euripides' iconoclastic hands – a treacherous, politically-crafty trimmer of an ambitious man. Such is the Master's sharply ironic portrait of a Homeric hero.

IPHIGENIA IN TAURIS   c. 414 BC

Iphigenia. Through the trickery of Odysseus I was brought to Aulis on pretext of marriage with Achilles. There I was seized for ritual sacrifice, and found myself upon the altar with the sharp sword over me about to strike, when the goddess Artemis rescued me, whisking me out of Grecian hands and leaving a deer in my place.

The goddess conveyed me through the radiant air to Tauris, where I would live in the land ruled by the barbarian king Thoas who appointed me priestess of the temple here. I am obliged to conduct the rites that Artemis delights in, and sacrifice any Greek whose ill fortune brings him to these shores.

DRAMATIS PERSONAE

Iphigenia,   daughter of Agamemnon and Clytemnestra,
            priestess of Artemis
Orestes, brother of Iphigenia
Pylades, friend of Orestes
Thoas, king of the Taurians
Herdsman
Messenger, servant of Thoas
The Goddess Athena
Chorus of Greek Women, captives, attendants of Iphigenia
                in the temple

Iphigenia in Tauris

This is a thorough and fine spoof, drawn close enough to the border of sobriety as to dupe the unwary. It stars an upbeat and stagemanaging Iphigenia as a priestess (she, a former victim). Orestes and Pylades arrive at this out-of-the-way place in the Crimea, sent by Apollo to steal an icon of Artemis. They are caught and narrowly miss being sacrificed by Iphigenia who has not seen her brother since he was a small child.

She and Orestes discover each other's identity in a famous recognition-scene (Aristotle liked it), and she contrives an escape for all of them from Tauris at the expense of an empty-headed tyrant who lays claim to the biggest-fool-of-the-year award. The climax finds the stern, clownish king Thoas locking himself in a temple where he cannot possibly see what goes on outside, a messenger pounding on the temple door and allowed by the king to speak for 77 lines explaining why no time should be lost in apprehending the escapees.

Concluding Comment

Even in the extremely comical *Iphigenia in Tauris* does Euripides inveigh against what he views as pernicious conceptions of the gods. That is, against seeing the gods as capable of vile behavior, and thus perhaps sanctioning men in their own illicit desires (meaning primarily, for Euripides, the violent aggressions involved in empire and war).

In our play here, the heroine Iphigenia forthrightly states the following:

> "I blame the false principles ascribed to the goddess Artemis, who forbids from her sacred altars anyone who has slain another, or so much as comes in contact with a dead body, or even assisted a pregnant woman in labor. Nevertheless, she herself takes pleasure in human sacrifice.
>
> [Euripides now speaks plainly about his countrymen.]
> "I do not believe these are the true principles of the goddess herself. No! Those humans who delight in slaughter shift their own guilt onto the goddess [i.e. use these conceptions of the gods as excuses and justifications]."

"I cannot believe that gods do evil or wrong."

Euripides also argued against superstition, employing parody and satire. The demagogues were fond of claiming favorable omens for their battle-ventures (Aristophanes burlesques this in *Knights*), which likely had a telling effect on the Athenians. They were highly superstitious and could see omens and portents everywhere.

Given such a situation, it was little wonder that the Athenians frequented Oracles. Euripides enjoyed joking about this, as in *Hippolytus* where (as mentioned previously) King Theseus returns from Delphi wearing a garland signifying the Oracle has glimpsed plenteous good luck in his future. Theseus arrives home to hear of the suicide of his beloved wife Phaedra, then trusts her deceitful letter upon which he kills his beloved son Hippolytus with a curse.

THE PHOENECIAN MAIDENS

c. 408 BC

Polyneices. Once again I ask you to give back to me my sceptre and rightful share in the kingdom.

Eteocles. I have nothing to return. This is my palace and I shall live in it.

Polyneices. What! Do you insist on having more than your fair share?

Eteocles. That's right, I do. Leave!

Alternate title: Latin, *Phoenissae*

DRAMATIS PERSONAE

Iocasta, wife of Oedipus (Latin, Jocasta)
Eteocles, now king of Thebes; son of Oedipus
Polyneices, exiled son of Oedipus; brother of Eteocles
Antigone, daughter of Oedipus
Old Servant, an attendant of Antigone
Creon, brother of Iocasta
Teiresias, the blind prophet
Menoeceus, son of Creon
First Messenger
Second Messenger
Oedipus, formerly king of Thebes
Daughter of Teiresias, guards, attendants
Chorus of Phoenecian Maidens

The Phoenecian Maidens

The Phoenecian Maidens re-tells the myth of Eteocles and Polyneices, the warring sons of Oedipus, which was the subject of Aeschylus in *Seven Against Thebes*. Euripides' tale accentuates the unrighteousness of Eteocles in retaining the Theban kingship, and also stresses the suffering to the innocent occasioned by strife and warface.

The inventive playwright keeps Oedipus and Iocasta alive to figure prominently in the tragedy, especially the latter. Iocasta tries to mediate between sons Eteocles and Polyneices in order to prevent the Seven Chiefs from attacking the city, and to give Polyneices his due share of royal power. She fails, and Euripides has her commit suicide over the bodies of the brothers mutually slain in single combat. Iocasta falls to the ground where her arms embrace the two of them, this latter symbolizing (with a touch of parody and/or melodrama) the tragedy of civil war.

Other important elements in the play: Eteocles' minister (and uncle) Creon inquires of the seer Teiresias for a means to save the city. The terrible oracle returned to him states that Creon's son Menoeceus must be ritually sacrificed. Creon arranges for his son to escape the city, but the honorable young man immolates himself. Upon the deaths of Eteocles and Polyneices, and the salvation of the city, the blind Oedipus sets out on his wanderings led by daughter Antigone. Creon's decree that Polyneices' corpse remain unburied leaves us with sure knowledge that the suffering will continue – after the finale of the play – with Antigone's martyred death.

The Phoenecian Maidens represents another Euripidean parable of the tragedy of the Greek civil war between Athens and Sparta. And, I think we can safely infer, Eteocles' arrogant lust for power was intended as the author's latest condemnation of Athens' imperialism which provoked the Peloponnesian War and prolonged it now into its third decade.

Concluding Comment

The ambitious, unscrupulous Eteocles makes a classic statement of Might is Right in the drama. He discourses,

> If all were at one in their ideas of honor and wisdom, there would have been no strife to make men disagree; but, as it is, fairness and equality have no existence in this world beyond the name. There is really no such thing. For instance, mother, I will tell thee this without any concealment; I would ascend to the rising of the stars and the sun, or dive beneath the earth, in order to win a monarch's power, the chief of things divine.

(506)

A cynic philospher, the contrary Antisthenes, once told a fable concerning a conference of the animal kingdom. The animals were discussing which system of government to devise. The rabbits put forward the notion of Equality, that everyone should have equal rights. The lions answered, "Equality? And just where are your claws and teeth?"

THE SUPPLIANTS   c. 419 BC

"Our presumption seeks to lord it over heaven, and in the pride of our hearts we think we are wiser than the gods. Methinks thou art even of this number, a son of folly, seeing that thou, though obedient to Apollo's oracle in giving thy daughters to strangers, as if gods really existed . . ." -- Theseus

Alternate title: Latin, *Supplices*

DRAMATIS PERSONAE

Chorus of Argive Mothers
Adrastus, king of Argos
Theseus, king of Athens
Aethra, mother of Theseus
Herald, of Creon, king of Thebes
Messenger
Evadne, wife of Capaneus (one of the Seven who fell
        before Thebes)
Iphis, father of Evadne
Children of the slain chieftains
The goddess Athena
Guards, attendants, soldiers

The Suppliants

This is a problematic play whose second half is not benignly plotted. That can occur when a dramatist concentrates on the messages he sends and considers his storyline to be a secondary matter.

The action takes up where Aeschylus' *Seven Against Thebes* concludes. Eteocles and Polyneices have slain one another. Creon becomes king of Thebes and forbids burial of the seven chiefs of the invading forces. King Adrastus of Argos and the Argive mothers of these Seven go to Athens. They plead with King Theseus to help them achieve burial for their sons.

Upholder of the righteous and punisher of the wicked, Theseus agrees to make war on Thebes, if necessary, to effect the panhellenic law of burial. A Theban herald arrives to debate with Theseus the merits of monarchy versus democracy, and peace versus the war Theseus has decided upon. The playwright has both men denounce rabblerousing demagogues. The Herald also issues a statement, which Euripides must have proffered seriously, pertaining to contemporary Athens and its empire: that Athens was a "meddler" in others' affairs. This was a fact.

The Athenian army attacks Thebes, and triumphs. Theseus magnanimously refrains from entering the beaten city, and saintly **washes** – he does it personally – the bloody wounds of dead Argive warriors.

The Athenians return to Athens (where the plot becomes somewhat episodic) with the corpses of the 7 fallen chiefs. A funeral procession and eulogy of each chief takes place there (commenting ironically on Aeschylus' martial eulogy of the 7 when living).

Then (believe it or not) Evadne, wife of Capaneus (one of the 7), actually leaps from a rock onto the burning funeral

185

pyre of her husband. (This melodrama, or parodying jest, is
an antiwar statement. It reinforces the antiwar irony of the
funeral eulogies.)

7 children, sons of the 7 chiefs, lament the loss of their
fathers. They ask the Chorus of Argive Mothers (their
grandmothers) if, when they are grown up, they should
avenge their fathers. Oh yes! say the mourning women.

Finally, the goddess Athena, protectress of Athens,
makes a *deus ex machina* appearance. She instructs King
Theseus to tell the children they must appreciate what
Athens has done for Argos, and have them vow on behalf of
all Argos to be Athens' loyal ally (as if children could bind
the nation!). They must also vow to take revenge on Thebes
once having grown up. Finis.

So what does this play mean? (1) It mocks Athenian
pretensions at benevolence. (For example, King Theseus
washing the wounds of dead foreign soldiers is great parody
and also satire.) (2) It damns the demagogues who forever
fueled Athenian war fever, and—as always—Euripides
damns the Peloponnesian War.

(3) The third antiwar message, the major and specific one
of the drama, concerns a treaty of alliance which Athens
had indeed recently concluded with Argos. Euripides
assails – with his customary irony – this treaty, because the
Peace of Nicias with Sparta was still in effect and Argos
was Sparta's enemy and rival in the Peloponnese. Sparta
would be sure to view the Athenian-Argive alliance as a
hostile act. So much for peace with Sparta, says Euripides
(and history).

When Athena (read Athens) tells the children to grow
up and attack Thebes (which was Sparta's important ally),

she was decreeing (Euripides predicting) the end of peace and a resumption of the Peloponnesian War. Of course, that's what happened, the War going on until 404 BC when Athens was defeated by Sparta.

Concluding Comment

I quote excerpts from Pericles' famous Funeral Oration. This was delivered after the conclusion of the first year of the Peloponnesian War in honor of the Athenians who had fallen thus far in battle. Pericles presents an idealized picture of Athens, but the quotation contains much that is true. He explicitly, or implicitly, compares Athens to Sparta (favorably to the Athenians, not surprisingly).

> "Let me say that our system of government does not copy the institutions of our neighbors. It is more the case of our being a model to others, than of our imitating anyone else. Our constitution is called a democracy because power is in the hands, not of a minority, but of the whole people."

> "When it is a question of settling private disputes, everyone is equal before the law. When it is a question of putting one person before another in positions of public responsibility, what counts is not membership of a particular class, but the actual ability which the man possesses. No one, so long as he has it in him to be of service to the state, is kept in political obscurity because of poverty."

> "Then there is a great difference between us and our opponents in our attitude towards military security. Here are some examples: Our city is open to the world, and we have no

periodical deportations in order to prevent people observing or finding out secrets which might be of military advantage to the enemy. This is because we rely, not on secret weapons, but on our own real courage and loyalty."

"There is a difference, too, in our educational systems. The Spartans, from their earliest boyhood, are submitted to the most laborious training in courage. We pass our lives without all these restrictions, and yet are just as ready to face the same dangers as they are."

"Our love of what is beautiful does not lead to extravagance. Our love of the things of the mind does not make us soft. We regard wealth as something to be properly used, rather than as something to boast about. As for poverty, no one need be ashamed to admit it."

"Here each individual is interested not only in his own affairs but in the affairs of the state as well. Even those who are mostly occupied with their own business are extremely well-informed on general politics – this is a peculiarity of ours. We do not say that a man who takes no interest in politics is a man who minds his own business; we say that he is good for nothing."

"This is another point where we differ from other people. We are capable at the same time of taking risks and of estimating them beforehand. Others are brave out of ignorance; and, when they stop to think, they begin to fear. But the man who can most truly be accounted brave is he who best knows the meaning of what is sweet in life and of what is terrible, and then goes out undeterred to meet what is to come."

(Thucydides, II. 37-40)

I believe that Pericles did speak the essential truth here – as far as it went. But he does not refer to the **moral character** of the people who manned the democracy. He does not, and could not criticize as unjust the policies of imperialism and war (since he was their principal architect).

Euripides **did** render such criticism. For a full discussion of the issues involved here, I might suggest reading **Socrates, The Martyred Messiah [an Essential History of Classical Athens]** by the present author.

THE HERACLEIDAE
(The Children of Hercules)

c. 429 BC

"I have firmly believed this for a long time: Nature created one man to be honest and upright for the benefit of those around him, while making another to be preoccupied with personal gain, a man useless to the State and difficult for people to deal with, but in his own opinion the very finest of men."

DRAMATIS PERSONAE

Iolaus, friend of Hercules
Demophon, king of Athens
Copreus, herald of Eurystheus
Eurystheus, king of Argos
Macaria, daughter of Hercules
Servant, of Hyllus, son of Hercules
Alcmene, mother of Hercules
Messenger
Chorus of Aged Athenians

The Heracleidae

The aged Iolaus, an old friend of the deceased Hercules, comes to Marathon (the site of Athens' epochal victory over the Persians) seeking sanctuary for the young sons of Hercules of whom he is the guardian. The king of Argos, Eurystheus (who gave Hercules the dangerous Labors to perform), wants their lives and intimidates any state which might consider giving them refuge.

The action-filled drama finds Eurystheus' remorseless herald, Copreus, knock the old man Iolaus to the ground, then attempt to seize the children of Hercules and tear them from the sacred altar of Zeus. The Chorus of Aged Athenians intervene, upholding the suppliants on moral and religious grounds. They are joined and supported by Demophon, the democratic king of Athens. Copreus threatens them with invasion from the mighty army of Argos, but Demophon will not back down, idealistically willing to risk his country for the sake of elementary morality; to wit, aiding helpless suppliants. The Argive herald leaves empty-handed but also leaves a credible warning behind him.

The Athenians prepare for war, the army of Argos does arrive, and Hercules' mature son Hyllus appears with a defending force. The Athenian seers advise that a young maiden must be ritually sacrificed to avoid defeat, but Demophon will not sacrifice a maid from Athens (unlike the non-democratic Argive king Agamemnon, the audience appreciates).

Macaria, a daughter of Hercules, comes forward to offer up herself so as to save her brothers and the city willing to fight for them. (Euripides, by the way, handles all this in a serious manner, no parody.) She is duly sacrificed before the Argive forces attack.

An admirable scene of comedy ensues as the geriatric Iolaus insists on donning armor and participating in the combat. The exchange between this feeble old man and the wry servant of Hyllus who seeks futilely to dissuade him is one fine stretch of humor (e.g. "Mere looks can wound no one," the servant quips). Finally armed and present on the battlefield, Iolaus prays for the return of one day of youth. This miraculously occurs, and he proceeds to demolish the enemy ranks and capture the evil and cowardly king Eurystheus.

The report of the above battle – miracle and all – was rendered without parody or satire, and the play is almost over. Where on earth is anti-war and anti-imperialism Euripides? The chauvinists and jingoists in the theatre are readying to applaud mightily when Euripides, at near the last moment, lowers the boom on them. Here is what he does:

The defeated king Eurystheus is brought, bound and yoked, before Hercules' mother Alcmene, grandmother of the Heracleidae. (Keep in mind that she is merely one of the refugees.) Alcmene abuses the king both verbally and physically, and demands his death. The Chorus – which represents Athenian citizenry – forthrightly declares it dishonorable and unlawful to execute an enemy who has been taken alive from the field of battle.

Eurystheus now speaks, and the man reported to be evil and cowardly shows himself anything but that. With courage and composure, bound and harnessed as he is, he explains that he had acted as Alcmene – and by inference anyone else in his position – would have done: he was safeguarding his throne and his life from vengeful, deadly rivals. The Athenian audience would surely have recognized the validity of the assertion.

Moreover, a sober spectator should recognize a further wisdom pronounced by Euristheus: Treat me unconscionably and you will receive like treatment from those who will imitate your behavior. This combines with something said previously by the Chorus when Demophon and Copreus were jousting : "It is forbidden to strike a herald!", which Demophon was about to do.

These two matters were intended to remind Euripides' audience of an atrocity they themselves had recently committed – the murder of Spartan ambassadors.

The drama draws to a close as Alcmene continues, brutally, to demand death, herself acting as if she were a prominent power in Athens. In her unbridled violence she even, vilely, orders the guards to throw the king's corpse to the dogs after execution. And here is the rub – What says the Chorus of Aged Athenians, these survivors of Marathon, representatives of the contemporary Athenian democracy?

"All right, we agree."

In other words and in summary, Euripides has pointed up a **contrast:** (a) the noble Athenian conduct of the past, especially in the Persian Wars – as dramatized by Chorus and King when protecting the suppliants, by Macaria's self-sacrifice and Iolaus' heroism, as opposed to (b) the moral corruption of contemporary Athens in murdering ambassadors, the condemnation of an entire population to death and slavery (Mytilene), and the uncompromising prosecution of a senseless war, in addition to sundry crimes and misdemeanors perpetrated by an imperial power against its subject states – as dramatized by Alcmene's brutality and the Chorus' treachery to ethics and law.

So that is the contrast Euripides holds up to his fellow citizens: the honor of the past, or continued moral debasement along the present lines.

The Heracleidae

Concluding Comment

The Heracleidae was set in Marathon. The Chorus was composed of Aged Athenians, meaning that they would remember what happened there in 490 BC and possibly were veterans of the battle. Athens, of course, won an epochal victory against the Persians.

These facts, together with Athens in Euripides' plot waxing triumphant over Thebes, permits the unwary to assume that the dramatist must have been writing a patriotic play. This assumption, however, collides with two fundamental problems. First, Euripides was the last person on earth to support military chauvinism. Second, references to Marathon can act as a chastisement to the wayward via a reminder of past glory.

At Marathon, Athens prevailed over the Persians, not over fellow Greeks. The Athenians fought in *defense* of their city, not involving themselves gratuitously in somebody else's feud.

One might recollect what Elpinice, the sister of deceased general and statesman Kimon, once said to Pericles, then the chief of state. Let Plutarch initially say something about this great man, Kimon, who repeatedly defeated the Persian Empire after Salamis and Plataea.

> After his death, no Greek general was to win another brilliant success against the barbarians. Instead, a succession of demagogues and warmongers arose [Plutarch greatly respected Pericles, yet he clearly includes him in this statement], who proceeded to turn the Greek

197

states against one another, and nobody could be found to separate or reconcile them before they met in the headlong collision of war.

("Kimon", 19)

In Plutarch's "Life" of Pericles, he wrote:

When Pericles returned home after subduing Samos, he had funeral honors paid to all the Athenians who had lost their lives in the campaign, and he won especial admiration for the speech he delivered over their tombs, according to the usual custom.

As he stepped down from the rostrum, many Athenian women clasped his hand and crowned him with garlands and fillets as if he were a victorious athlete. Elpinice, however, walked up to him and said: 'This was a noble action, Pericles, deserving garlands. You have thrown away the lives of our brave citizens, not in a war against Persians or Phoenecians, such as my brother Kimon fought, but in destroying a Greek city which is one of our allies.

(28)

HERCULES MAD date uncertain
c. 416 BC

Theseus. I cannot counsel you to die rather than to go on suffering. There is not a man alive that hath wholly escaped misfortune's taint, nor any god either, if what poets sing is true. Have they not intermarried in ways that law forbids? Have they not thrown fathers into ignominious chains to gain the sovereign power? Still they inhabit Olympus and brave the issue of their crimes.

Hercules. For my part, I do not believe that the gods indulge in unholy unions; and as for putting fetters on parents' hands, I have never thought that worthy of belief, nor will I now be so persuaded, nor again that one god is naturally lord and master of another. For the deity, if he be really such, has no wants. These are miserable fictions of the poets.

DRAMATIS PERSONAE

Hercules, son of Zeus and Alcmene
Amphitryon, husband of Alcmene, the mother of Hercules
Megara, wife of Hercules, daughter of Creon
Lycus, unlawful king of Thebes
Iris, a female deity serving the gods as messenger
Madness
Messenger
Theseus, king of Athens
Sons of Hercules, guards, attendants
Chorus of Old Men of Thebes

Hercules Mad

The fabulous hero, Hercules, has been away in Hades dragging the three-headed dog Kerberus to the surface of the planet. While he is so engaged, Lycus usurps the Theban throne from Creon and intends to kill Hercules' wife, parents and children in a blood feud. This parody of a tyrant struts around and needlessly drags out the time of execution until Hercules can return to rescue them. The dreadful despot finally revs himself up for the murders and, brimming with wicked joy, walks into Hercules. So much for the formidable King Lycus.

That parodying comedy was a clearly demarcated first half to the play. In the second part, Hercules delivers a loving speech on children just before he kills all of his, having been visited with a fit of madness by the goddess Hera. Back in his right senses, Hercules resolves on suicide. The hero Theseus, however, arrives to talk him out of it. Hercules should come to Athens where he may redeem himself. Hercules agrees.

Interpretation: View the parodying play symbolically. The first half -- Hercules slaying the despot -- represents Athens during its euphoric, independence-attaining, democracy-and-empire building days. The second half -- Hercules destroying his own family -- represents Greece and Athens destroying themselves.

Euripides introduced certain innovations in the Hercules-myth to create symbolism. He brought in Theseus to talk the hero out of committing suicide once his madness subsides, convincing the distraught legend he ought to redeem himself in Athens.

In this way, Euripides figuratively condemns the destructiveness of Athenian war policies, while encouraging an end to hostilities, redemption of the guilty, and renewed idealism.

Concluding Comment

Theseus was a mythical hero similar to Hercules in his exploits of courage and strength. (For instance, killing the Minotaur of Crete in the labyrinth.) As a youth, Theseus was said to admire the famous Hercules and wished to follow in his footsteps. The two slayers of terrible beasts, monsters, and wicked men would become friends.

According also to legend, Theseus was once king of Athens and united the region of Attica under Athens. The Athenians looked upon him as a lawgiver and grantor of democratic rights to the poor. At the festival in honor of Theseus, the Theseia, the poor people of the city-state received benedictions of meat and bread.

HELEN   412 BC

"My name is Helen, and I will now recount the sorrows I have suffered."

"Would God I could rub my beauty out like a picture, and assume hereafter in its stead a form less comely."

"Ah, woe is me!   who was ever more unfortunate than I?"

DRAMATIS PERSONAE

Helen, wife of Menelaus, king of Sparta
Menelaus
Teucer, a warrior who fought at Troy; half-brother of Ajax
Portress, of Theoclymenes
Theoclymenes, king of Egypt
Theonoe, sister of Theoclymenes
Servant, of Theoclymenes
First Messenger
Second Messenger
The Dioscuri, two gods who are brothers (Castor and
                        Polydeuces); Helen is their sister
Chorus of Captive Greek Women, attending Helen

Helen

Helen ought to be mock-dramatic enough for anyone to recognize (although this has seldom happened). The *casus belli* herself opens the play with a long tongue-in-cheek address telling of her divine transference from Troy to Egypt (the isle of Pharos to be specific), and how the ten-years war at Troy was fought over a phantom which looks like her. She modestly denies being attractive and cannot understand why anyone should fuss over her.

Helen deems herself the most woe-begotten of the woe-begotten. Not only do people blame her for what she did not do, but the Egyptian king holds her captive and won't let her go until she marries him. Imagine, this nasty business has been going on for ten years!

Husband Menelaus comes to town looking ragged and begging for food, leaving his wife (the phantom-Helen) aboard ship. Menelaus and Helen meet in the palace in which she remains a prisoner, eventually resolving the confusion of her resemblance to his wife. They make plans for a double-suicide (Don't ask why), choreographing the spectacle rather nicely but finally deciding against it. Instead, they live to escape, hoodwinking the king who is not much brighter than King Thoas of Tauris.

Concluding Comment

Euripides here tells a fanciful tale about Helen of Troy: that a phantom of Helen went to Troy and the woman herself travelled to Egypt. (Helen of Troy, therefore, was an **illusion**.)

The dramatist was adapting a story found in the lyric poetry of Stesichorus, 6th-century BC. This poet had written an earlier poem in which Homer's version of a Troy-absconding War-causing Helen was employed. Legend has it that Stesichorus was struck blind for having perpetuated such a "slander". Upon composing the second, phantom-esque poem, in the acclaimed *Palinode*, his eyesight was restored.

Surely, Stesichorus and those responsible for the blindness-legend are all guilty of a fine, trenchant, critical jest. To wit, 10 years of war over an adulterous woman was a heap of folly. Everyone involved was **blindly deluded**.

Ergo the Peloponnesian War, implies Euripides.

ORESTES   408 BC

Electra. After this, my poor Orestes fell sick of a cruel wasting disease. Upon his couch he lies prostrate, and it is his mother's blood that goads him into frenzied fits. This I say, from dread of naming those goddesses, whose terrors are chasing him before them.

DRAMATIS PERSONAE

Orestes, son of Agamemnon and Clytemnestra
Electra, sister of Orestes
Pylades, close friend of Orestes
Menelaus, king of Sparta
Helen, wife of Menelaus
Hermione, daughter of Menelaus and Helen
Messenger, formerly a servant of Agamemnon
A Phrygian Eunuch
The God Apollo
Tyndareus, father of Clytemnestra
Chorus of Argive Maidens

Orestes

We have another good spoof here. Euripides opens the play with a delectable portrait of the hero Orestes as a manic-depressive. Tormented by his conscience for having killed his mother, Orestes lies interminably on his couch trying desperately to sleep. This alternates with his jumping up to frantically pour out his woes to whomever stands within earshot. When he attempts to sleep, Electra warns the Chorus against speaking too loudly. The lower they speak, the more insistently Electra warns them. I would not be surprised if Euripides' stage direction had her shouting at them to be quiet, awakening poor Orestes with her clamor.

A mob-like assembly of citizens demands that brother and sister justify the matricide. Orestes and Pylades emerge from the palace and talk to the townsmen of Argos. Orestes and Electra are condemned to death but graciously permitted to commit suicide.

Orestes had previously asked his uncle Menelaus for help, but one look at the crowd outside and the great warrior, king of Sparta, offered words of consolation and excuse before slipping off. So, after the verdict, when Pylades suggests they kidnap and do away with Helen, Menelaus' wife, the idea is an audience-pleaser (although what good it will do them eludes me).

They kidnap Helen and are about to kill her when she miraculously disappears (a reminder of the Helen-phantom theme in *Helen* written four years earlier). Menelaus' and Helen's daughter Hermione shows up, allowing Orestes to put a sword to **her** throat. The substitution allows the god Apollo to make a *deus ex machina* appearance and order Orestes to drop the sword, and marry her instead. Then Apollo dictates an equally ridiculous marriage, a divorce, and an annulment of a marriage.

That ends the *Orestes*, with everyone going home happy except for literal and mirthless literary critics. Know that Euripides was having some fun. And incidentally informing his audience, by parodying gods and heroes, that violence and war are jests to be laughed at and **not** perpetrated.

Concluding Comment

Athenian dramatists frequently brought a god into the play by means of a "machine", a crane of some sort. This gave the appearance of the god having flown in from the sky. The term *deus ex machina* (Latin, "god from the machine") describes the introduction of a divine being in this way.

The notion of a *deus ex machina* tended over time, in literary criticism, to have a disparaging connotation. Why? Because gods and goddesses might be flown in at the denouement of the drama in order to resolve a conflict which critics believe should have been resolved by the characters themselves.

Euripides, particularly on account of the *Orestes*, has been associated with such an (allegedly) artificial plot resolution. Thus, subtle parodies, like gods and goddesses, often fly over our heads.

ANDROMACHE   c. 420 BC

Menelaus [speaking to Andromache, the
          enslaved widow of the slain Trojan
          hero Hector; Menelaus' attendants
          have just seized the noble woman].

It was to make thee leave the holy altar of the
goddess that I held thy child's death before thy
eyes, and so induced thee to give thyself up to
me to die. So stands thy case, be well assured.
But as for this child, my daughter shall decide
whether she will slay him or not. Get thee
hence into the house, and there learn to bridle
thy insolence in speaking to the free, slave that
thou art.

DRAMATIS PERSONAE

Andromache, widow of Hector, concubine-slave of
        Neoptolemus, the son of Achilles
Molossus, son of Andromache and Neoptolemus
Maid of Andromache
Hermione, daughter of Menelaus and Helen; wife of
        Neoptolemus
Menelaus, king of Sparta
Peleus, father of Achilles
Nurse of Hermione
Orestes, son of Agamemnon; nephew of Menelaus
Messenger
Thetis, a goddess, once the wife of Peleus
Chorus of Phthian Women

Andromache

This satirical takeoff on romance-literature stereotypes, perhaps simultaneously a melodrama, revolves around Andromache, widow of Hector. She has been enslaved by the Greeks and belongs to Neoptolemus, son of Achilles. Euripides depicts him as a good man who favors Andromache over his wife Hermione, daughter of Menelaus and Helen. The childless Hermione seethes with jealousy and wants to kill Andromache and the son she bore to Neoptolemus. Orestes seeks to marry Hermione who returns the desire, and Orestes successfully plots to have Neoptolemus killed at Delphi.

The task of slaying Andromache and son falls to Hermione's father Menelaus, king of Sparta, who willingly accepts. Orestes having been portrayed as a conniving assassin, the playwright now represents the *Iliad*'s hero as a blustering, cowardly murderer. Having de-romanticized Helen in other plays, the author's version of her daughter should not take one by surprise.

Old man Peleus, the father of Achilles and grandfather of Neoptolemus, arrives just-in-the-nick-of-time to stand between Menelaus and his purposed victims. Unarmed, he faces down the vanquisher of myriad Trojans, who slinks away leaving empty threats in his wake.

The caricaturing story receives a *deus ex machina* appearance from the widower Peleus' deified wife Thetis. Peleus had been lamenting his lonely, pitiable state, and she descends to cheer him up with news that he too will be deified to live happily ever after. The mock-wonder Chorus has the last lines, observing dryly how regularly the unexpected takes place.

Concluding Comment

The chief villain of *Andromache* is Menelaus, king of Sparta. He sets about to murder the heroine and her child.

The Peloponnesian War had been underway for some 12 years by the time this drama was staged. A casual interpretation would view the author as playing to the grandstand, painting Sparta as an ogre through the nasty figure of Menelaus.

Such could not possibly be true of **Euripides**, the devoted adversary of Athenian imperialism and war policy. I suggest that something else, which occurred soon before *Andromache* was produced, an immense tragedy and evil, may afford insight into what prompted Euripides' real concern.

Ever since the Mytilenian Debate of 427, a Damocles sword had been hanging over the head of any subject state which revolted against Athens. In 423, Scione rebelled, and in 421 the Athenians crushed the revolt and condemned the population. Thucydides writes simply:

> The Athenians subjected Scione during this summer [421 BC]. They put to death all males of military age, enslaved the women and children, and awarded the land to the Plataeans.

Therefore, Menelaus, nominally a Spartan in *Andromache,* represents people closer to home who would favor the most brutal crimes against the helpless.

Andromache

Euripides' *Hecuba*, and the background of tragic events in Greece, evoke a philosophical statement by the immortal Socrates (found in Plutarch's *Moralia*). Socrates professed, regarding the human inclination to worry and pity oneself: If everyone brought his troubles and placed them in a common store to be distributed equally, most would be content to take back their own troubles and go home.

ION   c. 410 BC

Ion. Yet must I blame the god, if thus perforce
    He mounts the bed of virgins, and by stealth
    Becomes a father, leaving then his children
    To die, regardless of them. Do not thou
    Act thus; but, as thy power is great, respect
    The virtues; for whoe'er, of mortal men,
    Dares impious deeds, him the gods punish. How
    Is it then just that you, who gave the laws
    To mortals, should yourselves transgress those
    Laws?

DRAMATIS PERSONAE

The God Hermes
Creusa, princess of Athens
Ion, son of Creusa and the god Apollo, sacristan at
    Apollo's temple in Delphi
Xuthus, husband of Creusa
Old Retainer of Creusa
Servant of Creusa
Priestess of Apollo
The Goddess Athena
Attendants of the Temple of Apollo
Chorus of Creusa's Handmaidens

Ion

The drama adapts the legend of Ion, the Ancestor of the Ionian people. (The islands of Ionia are located east of Greece proper in the Aegean Sea of Asia Minor.)

The god Apollo impregnates a princess of Athens, Creusa, who gives birth to a boy (Ion), abandoning him in a cave. The messenger-god Hermes saves the babe and deposits him at Apollo's temple in Delphi where he is cared for and grows up to work as a temple attendant.

Ion's mother Creusa one day comes to Delphi and eventually discovers the true identity of the youthful attendant. Before the recognition, however, she tries to poison Ion out of jealousy, wrongly believing him to be her husband's son by a concubine. After recognition, Ion leaves with his parents for Athens.

Interpretation: The play concludes at this point. According to the myth, Ion will become king of Athens and the original ancestor of the Greeks who will populate Ionia.

Ion's storyline is very much in the folk-tale mode, the foundling tradition. Certainly a well-told tale, it must also convey an important political or social message, otherwise Euripides would not have written it. What does Euripides intend?

First, he clearly disparages Apollo and paints an unidyllic picture of the genesis of an Athenian king who fathered Ionia. The Ionian states will fall under Athenian suzerainty in the Delian League empire.

Interpret the play as an attempt to undermine the mythical justification (propaganda) for the Athenian empire, for Athens' imperialistic hold on the Ionian states. This hold could be quite brutal, and was always – its raison d'etre – financially exploitative.

And, on the authority of Thucydides, Athens' empire was the principal cause of the Peloponnesian War. Sparta's fear of Athens, due to the existence of that empire, triggered the war which had lasted 13 years when Euripides presented *Ion* at the Dionysian festival.

Therefore, view the drama as an attack on the many injustices perpetrated by Athens on its "allies" (subject states), and another effort by Euripides to bring peace to the land – this by dissolving, or at least reducing – the major cause of the War, Athenian imperialism.

Ion

Concluding Comment

Ion has a different tone from any other play we have of Greek Drama. Clearly it was one of those works which influenced the formation of post-classical New Comedy. Associated principally with the dramatist Menander, the New Comedy involved stories of "human interest" and "manners", social and family situations, romances. It was apolitical, most unlike the Old Comedy of Aristophanes and his confreres. One good reason for this: Athens had by this time been subjugated by Macedonia. Serious mordant political or social comment was forbidden on the stage.

The reader will discover themes in *Ion* which will appear in New Comedy, themes familiar to our tradition of folk- and fairy tales. Most prominent is the foundling-motif: the long-lost child grows to adulthood, is finally recognized, and general felicity results.

This variety of the foundling-motif differs markedly from the foundling aspect of the Oedipus legend (and that of the Trojan prince, Paris). There, the babe Oedipus is abandoned to die, is saved and grows up into fame and power. But what transpires after that bears no resemblance to New Comedy. The dissimilarity emblemizes, in a way, the difference between the Arts in Classical Athens and what they would become after the Spartan conquest. The Athenians would regain their independence, and their democratic institutions. Yet, fourth-century Athens would pale before the golden age of the Arts in the fifth century. Even an Aristotle could not come near bridging the distance.

ALCESTIS   438 BC

"Will none come forth?
Must I shear my hair?
Must we wrap ourselves
In black mourning folds?"

DRAMATIS PERSONAE

Alcestis, the queen, wife of Admetus
Admetus, king of Thessaly
Hercules
The God Apollo
Death
A Woman Servant
A Man Servant
Eumelus, son of Admetus and Alcestis
Pheres, father of Admetus
Chorus of Old Men

Alcestis

This is one of the best comedies ever composed, a joshing romance with all the charm in the world. The first part of the play counterfeits tragedy. The dying, gasping and gagging Queen Alcestis wheedles a promise out of her husband Admetus never to re-marry. King Admetus' self-pitying, histrionic miseries take off on the interesting fact that he had invited her to die as a favor to him. (A choice morsel: Cutting off a lock hair was a sign of mourning. In honor of his wife's memory, Admetus vows to shave the mane off every horse in the kingdom.)

Admetus and Alcestis put on quite a mock-tragic show. Nonetheless, the stellar attraction of the play is Hercules, a rollicking and warm-hearted madcap. He comes to the palace of his friend, King Admetus, unaware that the virtuous Queen Alcestis has just died. Despite what should have been a comprehensible hint that the house was in mourning and the time was not propitious to come visiting, Hercules does not take the hint. The great champion jauntily explains that he is on his way to another heroic labor, quips about the perils of bridling horses that breathe fire, and insists that he be wined and dined before engaging upon his exploit. The annoyed Servant calls the distraught King to speak with his friend.

Admetus, obviously in mourning, says the loved one was close to him, not stating plainly that it was Alcestis who died. Hercules offers to go elsewhere for his victuals, but the King will not let him, insisting he stay. The servants will care for him in another room while Admetus proceeds with the funeral service for "a close friend of the family".

What happens now produces a comic situation to marvel at. The bereaved King argues over the casket with his own father while Hercules wines and dines elsewhere.

The background to the argument: King Admetus was slated to die, but the god Apollo would save him from the King of Death if Admetus can find a substitute. The King asked around but there were no bidders. His father and mother refused, and upon that refusal Admetus' wife Alcestis promised to die in her husband's stead. Admetus allowed her to do this, and now he shouts over her coffin at his father for having "killed" his wife by refusing to die in his son's place. His father shouts back that everyone has to look out for himself, that he gave Admetus life, the kingship, and a lot of money – what else could he ask for? Admetus replies that his father and mother are old, and at least one of them should have been willing to do him one last favor. After all, "I am your only son."

As this singular quarrel goes on, Hercules sits in another room stuffing himself and drinking them out of house-and-home. Soon he puts a garland on his head and sings drunkenly, yelling for servants to bring more food and wine. The Servant is loyal to his master, loved his deceased mistress, is a prim, censorious type and up-to-his-chin with indignation against Hercules. Meanwhile, the argument over the coffin continues until the father hurls a parting epithet at his son, the King, and stomps out of the palace.

Hercules learns from the Servant that Alcestis has died. He excuses himself "for a while", leaving the palace. The Servant had previously fired off a scathing soliloquy against the hero. But Hercules happens to be "a figure of conscience, honesty, and faithful service" replete with "sympathy, warmth and energy of mind". We have seen the roistering aspect of his character, now he shows us the exemplary man with the muscle and will to do great good.

Alcestis

The hero goes out on an errand, a Labor to be sure. He explains his mission to us:

Come, heart and hand, your endless endurance must be put to test! Now show what sort of son Alcmene of Tiryns bore to immortal Zeus! The woman's dead; and I must rescue her, and pay the debt of kindness I owe Admetus by setting Alcestis in her own home again -- alive!

That black-robed King of the Dead will come to drink the blood of victims offered at her tomb. That's where I'll find him. I'll hide there, watch for him, leap out and spring on him; once I have my arms locked round his writhing ribs, there's no power on earth shall wrench him free, till he gives her up to me!

What if I miss my prey, if the bait of blood fails to fetch him? Then I'll go down to the sunless palace of Persephone and her King and ask for her; and, by my soul, I shall bring Alcestis up again and deliver her safe into Admetus' hands,--my true friend, who, sooner than send me away, even at a time of mortal sorrow, out of pure nobleness and love for me, hid his distress and received me as a guest in his house. Is there a heart more generous in Thessaly, in Hellas itself?

He shall not say that his kindness was
shown to an ungrateful friend.

Hercules delivers. The final scene of the play, when
the hero presents a veiled, silent Alcestis to her husband,
was employed by Shakespeare when he composed the
Statue-scene for *The Winter's Tale.*

Concluding Comment

Alcestis was presented as a satyr-play following a trilogy of tragic poetic dramas. One ought to remember this fact when tempted to think the first part of the story to be bonafide tragedy. The parodying initial part attaches itself nicely to the manifestly comic, Herculean second half.

It is interesting that the dramatist would employ *Alcestis* as a satyr-play. His other extant example of the genre, *Cyclops*, was plainly in the burlesquing, satyric mode. Euripides, however, was a highly original, ingenious writer who demonstrated his flexibility and dexterity in many different ways.

THE CYCLOPS   date uncertain

Cyclops (*to Odysseus*).   Now tell me stranger,
                  by what name to call thee.
Odysseus. Noman. What boon shall I receive of thee
        to earn my thanks [for making wine]?
Cyclops. I will feast on thee last, after all thy comrades.
Odysseus. Fair indeed the honor thou bestowest on
        thy guest, sir Cyclops.
Cyclops (*turning suddenly to Silenus, leader of the satyrs*).
        Ho, sirrah! What art thou about? Taking
        a stealthy pull at the wine?
Silenus.   No, it kissed me for my good looks.
Cyclops.   Thou shalt smart, if thou kiss the wine
        when it kisses not thee.
Silenus.   Oh! But it did, for it says it is in love
        with my handsome face.

DRAMATIS PERSONAE

Silenus, old servant of the Cyclops
Odysseus
The Cyclops
Companions of Odysseus
Chorus of Satyrs

The Cyclops

Cyclops is quite unique, the only complete satyr-play comedy capping the Dionysian festival's tragic trilogy to have survived from classical Greece. It burlesques the Cyclops episode of the *Odyssey* and features tippling, wisecracking satyrs who one-up both Cyclops and Odysseus alike.

Silenus, leader of the satyrs, an enthusiastic imbiber and an artful dodger, is actor enough to blame the wily Odysseus for the theft of cheese and sheep, and get away with it. The Chorus of satyrs adroitly mock the Cyclops -- their slaver -- and Silenus double-talks him while stealing quaffs of the ogre's liquor.

The satyrs had all along talked big about helping Odysseus put out the Cyclops' eye. When the time has come to act, they develop back pains:

> Because I feel for my back and spine, and
> express no wish to have my teeth knocked
> out, I am a coward, am I?

They have their cake and eat it too. Odysseus and his men take the risks, and the satyrs reap the benefits -- wine, safety, and escape.

Concluding Comment

The clever Silenus, closely associated with the Chorus of Satyrs, was not actually a satyr, although he looked like one. On Attic vases, he appears as primarily a man but with ears, legs or tail of a horse. (A centaur would have the entire body of a horse.) Satyrs also appeared human, in the main, often with the legs of a goat.

The major difference between Silenus and a satyr was personality. The latter species were lustful, boisterous, revelling drinkers who gambolled in the woods and hills. They represented the animal traits of human beings.

Silenus, in contrast, was a sagacious fellow, indeed a wise man with an unusual, satyr-like physique. The story goes that King Midas learned his golden touch from Silenus. When the exuberant Midas became aghast at what happened to his very food when touched, the sage Silenus also taught him how to lose "the Midas touch".

Socrates was said to bear a striking resemblance to Silenus, respecting portraiture and mentality alike. Their unprepossessing, ugly exteriors encased mines of inner wisdom.

Conclusion

EURIPIDES -- No summing up can do justice to the idealism and artistry of this dramatic poet. Perhaps the best tribute was paid by Plutarch, whose respects included an astounding 225 direct quotations from Euripides in Plutarch's renowned *Moral Sayings*. If ever there were a means of recommending an author which supersedes such mammoth quotation, Plutarch managed it in his "Life" of Nicias (a chapter from his *Lives of the Noble Grecians and Romans*). He writes of the Athenians' disastrous invasion of Sicily, and of the imprisonment of the vanquished:

> XXIX. Most of the Athenians perished in the stone quarries of disease and evil fare, their daily rations being a pint of barley meal and a half-pint of water; but not a few were stolen away and sold into slavery, or succeeded in passing themselves off for servingmen. These, when they were sold, were branded in the forehead with the mark of a horse,-- yes, there were some freemen who actually suffered this indignity in addition to their servitude.

> But even these were helped by their restrained and decorous bearing; some were speedily set free, and some remained with their masters in positions of honour.

> Some also were saved for the sake of Euripides. For the Sicilians, it would seem,

more than any other Hellenes outside the home land, had a yearning fondness for his poetry. They were forever learning by heart the little specimens and morsels of it which visitors brought them from time to time, and imparting them to one another with fond delight.

In the present case, at any rate, they say that many Athenians who reached home in safety greeted Euripides with affectionate hearts, and recounted to him, some that they had been set free from slavery for rehearsing what they remembered of his works; and some that, when they were roaming about after the final battle, they had received food and drink for singing some of his choral hymns.

Surely, then, one need not wonder at the story that the Caunians, when a vessel of theirs would have put in at the harbour of Syracuse to escape pursuit by pirates, were not admitted at first, but kept outside, until, on being asked if they knew any songs of Euripides, they declared that they did indeed, and were for this reason suffered to bring their vessel safely in.

And I can only repeat my own admiration for the brilliant and original Euripides.

ARISTOPHANES

The bawdy, burlesquing, biting
Master of political comedy

circa
(445-380 BC)

This great master of burlesque and lampoon, parody and satire, this "court jester, moral crusader, social uplifter, philosopher, poet" applied his supreme comic talents to practically every subject of topical importance to the Athenian citizen. He pilloried politicians, jeered at the courts, derided sophistry and Socrates, boosted Aeschylus and parodied-hooted at Euripides, denounced war and promoted free trade and farming, damned city corruptions and hailed the clean country life.

Aristophanes rollicked his way impudently and bawdily, wittily and riotously yet seriously and lyric-poetically through all of it. He had a running public battle with the popular demagogue Cleon, who put him on trial. Aristophanes did not hesitate to speak out freely before his acquittal or after it.

When Dionysius of Syracuse asked Plato to explain the Athenian constitution, the great philosopher sent him the comedies of Aristophanes. When the dramatic poet died, Plato wrote this epitaph:

The Graces, seeking an imperishable sanctuary,
found the soul of Aristophanes.

A Note on Organization
of the Plays in this Chapter

(1) *The Acharnians, Peace, Lysistrata*: These 3 peace-anti-war plays are in chronological order by date of composition.

(2) *Knights* and *Wasps* are anti-Cleon (the demagogue) comedies in chronological order by date of composition.

(3) *Clouds* – a satire on Socrates.

(4) *Thesmophoriazusae* and *Frogs* involve Euripides (in parody), and are arranged in chronological order by date of composition.

(5) *Birds* and *Ecclesiazusae* are utopian comedies, ordered chronologically by date of composition.

(6) *The Plutus* is the last extant play we have from Aristophanes, and near the last one he composed. Contrary to ordinary critical opinion, I deem it a brilliant play and a fabulous late entry in a fabulous career.

THE ACHARNIANS 425 BC

The Pnyx was a hill near the Acropolis where
the Assembly of Athenian citizens met to discuss
public affairs and legislate. Dicaeopolis goes
there to demand an end to the Peloponnesian
War. He is the first to arrive.

"They will never trouble themselves with the
question of peace. Oh! Athens! Athens! As
for myself, I do not fail to come here before all
the rest, and now, finding myself alone, I groan,
yawn, stretch, fart, and know not what to do. I
make sketches in the dust, pull out my loose
hairs, muse, think of my fields, long for peace,
curse town life and regret my dear country home
. . . I have come to the assembly fully prepared
to bawl, interrupt and abuse the speakers, if they
talk of anything but peace."

DRAMATIS PERSONAE

Dicaeopolis, an old farmer
Herald
Amphitheus, an immortal
Ambassadors, recently returned from the Persian Court
Pseudartabas, envoy of the Great King (of Persia)
Theorus, ambassador to the king of Thrace
Wife of Dicaeopolis
Daughter of Dicaeopolis
Euripides, the tragedian
Cephisophon, servant of Euripides
Lamachus, a general
Attendant of Lamachus
A Megarian
Two Young Girls, daughters of the Megarian (disguised as
                        piglets)
A Boeotian
An Informer
A Farmer
A Bridesmaid
Nicarchus, another informer
Messengers
Chorus of Acharnian Elders

Dicaeopolis, an ordinary citizen sick-and-tired of the Peloponnesian War, comes to the Assembly on the Pnyx demanding that peace be made. Despite his best and most determined, obnoxious efforts to promote the cause, he goes away emptyhanded.

Undeterred, our hero concludes a private peace with Sparta, to the dismay of warmongers like Lamachus, Western literature's original *miles gloriosus*. (Dolon of Euripides' *Rhesus* might be the first; although Lamachus serves as a classic example of the military-braggart genre.)

Lamachus is not welcome at the private market Dicaeopolis opens, at which victims of the war policy **are** welcome. A visitor wishes to purchase an authentic Athenian product, and Dicaeopolis sells him an **informer**.

A comedy of comparison between warlike pursuits and peacetime pleasures finishes for Lamachus in ludicrous and ignoble fashion. An attentant of Lamachus announces the battle-scarred veteran's return:

> In leaping a ditch, the master has hurt himself against a stake; he has dislocated and twisted his ankle, broken his head by falling on a stone. His mighty braggadocio plume rolled on the ground; at this sight he uttered these doleful words; "Radiant star, I gaze on thee for the last time; my eyes close to all light, I die."

In contrast, Dicaeopolis makes his final entrance tipsy with wine, a courtesan on each arm, and singing merrily: Oh! My gods! What breasts! Swelling like quinces! Come, my treasures, give me voluptuous kisses!

Concluding Comment

Aristophanes' Dicaeopolis, whose name means "Honest Citizenry", is a vital, insistent, irrepressible, and inventive democratic figure if ever one existed. Athens' participatory democracy encouraged such a person to assert his views, his rights, his "day in court", and his days in the actual administration of the governement.[1]

Participatory democracy presupposed that a multitude of citizens would in fact participate in the Assembly sessions. (Duty and positions in the executive and judiciary spheres were normally designated by lot.) Human nature being what it was and is, many preferred to stay in the marketplace rather than sit and deliberate in the *Ecclesia* on the Pnyx. Dicaeopolis says, in the beginning of the play, when he is the first to arrive at the Assembly,

> It is the day of assembly. All should be here at daybreak, and yet the Pnyx is still deserted. They are gossiping in the marketplace, slipping hither and thither to avoid the vermilioned rope.

What the dallying and loitering citizens sought to avoid was a rope freshly painted red used to round up on Assembly days those malingerers and recalcitrants still in the Agora (marketplace). The red paint on their white robes identified them to officials who levied a fine on the red-striper.

---

[1] All free-born male citizens possessed the right to vote and act in the government. Women, foreign residents, and slaves did not have these rights.

By the way, on Athenian who took no interest in public affairs was called an **idiotes,** whence ultimately derived our word "idiot".

PEACE 421 BC

Peace is an exalted theme and Aristophanes persistently fought for it. He knew the value of his pursuit and the worth of the dramatist who did the pursuing.

Chorus. Oh Muse, if it be right to esteem the most honest and illustrious of our comic writers at his proper value, permit our poet to say that he has deserved a glorious renown. [mentions a few impertinencies of other playwrights] After having delivered us from all these wearisome ineptitudes and these low buffooneries, he has built up for us a great art, like a palace with high towers, constructed of fine phrases, great thoughts and of jokes not common on the streets.

Moreover, it's not obscure private persons or women that he stages in his comedies; but, bold as Hercules, it's the very greatest whom he attacks.

DRAMATIS PERSONAE

Trygaeus
Two Servants of Trygaeus
Daughter of Trygaeus
Hermes
War
Turmoil (or Riot, Tumult)
Hierocles, a Soothsayer
A Sickle-Maker
A Crest-Maker
A Breastplate-Maker
A Trumpet-Maker
A Helmet-Maker
A Spear-Maker
Son of Lamachus (the father was a general, depicted as a
            warmonger in *The Acharnians*)
Son of Cleonymus (the father was notorious for having
            thrown away his shield at the battle of
            Delium so he could flee the quicker)
Chorus of Farmers

Peace

This is the second of the peace-plays we possess from Aristophanes. *The Acharnians* was written in 425 BC, winning first prize at the Lenaean festival. *Peace* gained the second prize at the Great Dionysia in 421. (A dramatist named Eupolis came in first with a lost work, *The Flatterers,* another reminder of how much has failed to come down to us.)

The bellicose demagogue Cleon was a victim of the battlefield in 422. When Aristophanes composed *Peace* the following year, he may have been more hopeful of pacific negotiations with Sparta than at any time in the past 10 years.

From the Dramatis Personae can be seen the War-Antiwar contrasts: Son of Lamachus (the military braggart of *The Acharnians*) and Son of Cleonymus (a notorious and real-life battlefield coward; Aristophanes lauds Cleonymus as "excellent in military matters"). In another opposition we have War, Turmoil, A Crest-Maker, A Breastplate-Seller, A Trumpeter, A Helmet-Seller versus the Chorus of Farmers and A Sickle-Maker.

As the action initiates, two slaves of the hero Trygaeus are seen feeding excrement to a giant beetle. Trygaeus, like Dicaeopolis before him, has come to the conclusion that only the most creative, extraordinary efforts will bring about the coveted peace. His scheme: fly to heaven on his well-fueled dung-beetle (a parody of the flying horse Pegasus) and petition directly the king of the gods, Zeus.

Trygaeus takes off and the beetle gets him there. At the celestial palace, he hears that the gods are fed up with the Greeks and have washed their hands of them. Mortal affairs have been left in the (unclean) hands of War and his slave Turmoil.

The merciless War has consigned Peace to the bottom of a rock-filled pit. War has a gigantic mortar in which he plans to grind up Greece. Once he has obtained a pestle, War will begin his grisly task.

The destroyer loses time casting about for a pestle. Trygaeus seeks to take advantage of the opportunity to excavate Peace from Her pit. Farmers and workers from the various regions of Greece arrive to assist him. Despite setbacks occasioned by the shortcoming peculiar to each Greek state, and thanks primarily to the Farmers (Aristophanes was a landowning agriculturalist), Trygaeus succeeds in his mission.

Peace

Concluding Comment

Aristophanes presented *Peace* at the Great Dionysia in the spring of 421 BC. Unlike the earlier production of *The Acharnians*, and the later *Birds* and *Lysistrata* -- all specifically antiwar plays -- the occasion for *Peace* was one of fond hope for a conclusion to the Peloponnesian War. Peace did indeed seem at hand as serious negotiations between Athens and Sparta were taking place during the period of *Peace*'s gestation and presentation.

A particular event had fostered high hope: the battle of Amphipolis in which the major warmonger on each side had participated and actually been killed. Cleon, the violent Athenian demagogue, and the all-too capable Spartan general, Brasidas, engaged in a battle which cost them their lives. (Hence, in the play, War temporarily has lost his **pestle**.)

With Cleon and Brasidas dead, Aristophanes quickly composed and then staged **Peace** at the festival. It won second prize in the comedy competition. And soon thereafter, the Peace of Nicias brought a welcome (if temporary) cessation to hostilities between Sparta and Athens.

LYSISTRATA 411 BC

A woman determines to
wage war against The War.

Lysistrata. Greece saved by the women! Our country's fortunes depend on us.

Kalonike. But how should women perform so wise and glorious an achievement, we women who dwell in the retirement of the household, clad in diaphanous garments of yellow silk and long flowing gowns, decked out with flowers and shod with dainty little slippers?

Lysistrata. Ah, but those are the very sheet-anchors of our salvation -- those yellow tunics, those scents and slippers, those cosmetics and transparent robes.

DRAMATIS PERSONAE

Lysistrata, an Athenian woman, become leader of the
          peace-loving Women of Hellas (Greece)
Kalonike and Myrrhine, Athenian women
Lampito, a Spartan woman
Stratyllis, leader of the Chorus of Women
A Magistrate
Scythian Policemen
Kinesias, husband of Myrrhine
A Child, of Kinesias and Myrrhine
Herald of the Spartans
Envoys of the Spartans
Polycharides, an Athenian negotiator
Market Idlers
Doorkeeper of the Acropolis
An Athenian Citizen
Chorus of Old Men
Chorus of Women

Lysistrata

A strong-willed Athenian woman can no longer tolerate the War without waging war upon it. She calls a meeting of women from various parts of Greece, in particular a friend from Sparta, to tell them of a plan she conceived to bring the war to a close.

The women arrive, confer, and agree to her plan. They take a solemn oath never again to have sexual intercourse with their husbands and lovers until Peace has been made.

They seize the Acropolis, along with its Treasury which supplies war needs. The women proceed to honor their pledge. Both male and female are seized by their sexual needs, but the women have more endurance. After many bawdy references and near-incidents, the men surrender.

Lysistrata, attended by her handmaiden Reconciliation, mediates a Peace conference between Athens and Sparta, everyone partaking of a peace-victory banquet. Then all pair up and exeunt to gratify their desires.

Concluding Comment

The occupation of the Acropolis by representatives of the women of Greece is a central focus of the plot. Let us mention a few facts about the Acropolis, a famous place in antiquity which is one of the world's foremost tourist attractions today.

Literally "high" or "upper" (**acro**) "town", "city", "city-state" (**polis**), it was the citadel of Athens. A plateau some 200 feet in height, 1000 feet east-west and 500 feet north-south, the Acropolis constituted a fortress because of its defense potential. It became a religious center containing a number of temples, the most notable being the Parthenon (Temple of the Maiden, signifying the goddess Athena who was the city's special protectress).

The Parthenon, 10 years in the building (447 BC until its dedication in 438), was part of a vast program of statues and temples instituted by Pericles. Its construction was under the supervision of a highly celebrated sculptor, who himself crafted the great statue of Athena located inside the exquisitely-lined Parthenon. This sculptor was Phidias, whose renown in ancient times as an artist may be compared to that of Michelangelo in the Renaissance.

One more item, about fauna. Athens was home to an extremely large number of owls. Townsmen had an expression, "to bring owls to Athens" -- as bringing coals to Newcastle.

Lysistrata

A contingent of owls went to perch on the Acropolis at night. Their hooting, causing sleeplessness, was one of the complaints filed by the heroic occupiers to generalissimo Lysistrata when the going got tough.

KNIGHTS 424 BC

"We have a very brutal master, a perfect glutton for beans [used for casting votes in legal cases], and most bad-tempered; it's Demos of the Pnyx, an intolerable old man and half deaf. The beginning of last month he bought a slave, a Paphlagonian tanner, an arrant rogue, the incarnation of slander. This man of leather knows his old master thoroughly. He plays the fawning cur, flatters, cajoles, wheedles, and dupes him at will with little scraps of leavings which he allows him to get."

DRAMATIS PERSONAE

Demos, an old man, typifying the Athenian people
Paphlagon, a bullying slave of Demos who dominates the
    Master, representing the demagogue Cleon
Demosthenes and Nicias, Slaves of Demos, in opposition to
    Paphlagon, representing two contemporary
    generals of Athens
A Sausage-Seller, Agoracritus
Chorus of Knights

Knights

Knights is a comic satire/political allegory in which the master Demos (i.e. the Athenian populace) finds himself manipulated by a newly acquired slave, Paphlagon (i.e. the demagogue Cleon). Paphlagon is a clever, shifty, self-serving rogue who flatters, fawns, hoodwinks, controls, and fleeces Demos.

Two other slaves (with names of accomplished generals recently victimized by Cleon), oppressed by Paphlagon, urge a Sausage-Seller to compete with him for Demos' favor. ("Sausage" likely has a second, obscene meaning.) After all, the Sausage-Seller has everything necessary to enter the (political) arena -- inexperience, ignorance, low birth, impudence, and dishonesty.

The Sausage-Seller and the Paphlagonian meet and slug it out, exchanging loud, boisterous, and insolent demagogic accusations and threats. The Sausage-Seller wins, not via any righteous appeal, but by outdoing him at his own vile game. Demos returns to glory after the Paphlagonian's fall, and Paphlagon (remember he signifies Cleon) receives his punishment -- forced to sell sausages in the red-light district.

Concluding Comment

After the death of Pericles, Athenian leadership lost all moderation. Demagogues gained the adherence of the populace, in particular the "violent" (Thucydides' apt word) Cleon.

First, the term "demagogue" originally signified "leader of the people". Owing to Cleon and kindred spirits (such as his follower Hyperbolus), "demagogue" eventually came to mean a rabblerouser, one who appealed to people's base and worst instincts.

Cleon, a tanner of hides by trade (or owner of such a business) before entering politics, was an exceptionally effective speaker. This was the key to his dominance in the Assembly. His rhetoric was violent. His purposes were violent. The methods he urged were violent.

The Greeks wore robes which lent dignity while impeding movement. Cleon hitched up his clothes. Waving his arms wildly, he demanded war and opposed any peace resolution. He demanded that any subject state in the empire to revolt should be wiped out, literally. He was responsible for the Mytilean decree which condemned the city. It was rescinded in spite of him, but the precedent had been set. Scione and Melos would suffer the mass slaughter and enslavement proposed for Mytilene.

Cleon appealed to mercenary interests. War and victory brought money and land to divide up. If they wanted these things -- as was only sensible -- they had to crush opposition and seize the spoils. As he put it so simplistically and cutely during the Mytilenian Debate,

The only alternative is to surrender your empire, so that you can afford to go in for philanthropy.

Cleon held certain principles to be inviolable: 1. Might is Right. 2. The End justifies the Means. 3. Power and Money are everything; Virtue means nothing. Read, in Thucydides (Book III), Cleon's shrewdly anti-intellectual, brutal speech in support of Mytilene's destruction. Interesting and instructive.

Aristophanes criticized Cleon in the dramatist's second play in competition, *The Babylonians,* which has not survived. It may have won the first prize. The demagogue used his power in an attempt to suppress the critic, but failed. From this time on, the ruthless politician had no more courageous and persistent an opponent than the comic poet, Aristophanes.

WASPS   422 BC

A juror, to condemn a man on trial,
could trace a horizontal line across
a waxen tablet, or drop a pebble in
the conviction-urn.

"To be judging is his hobby, and he groans if
he is not sitting on the first seat. . . .
He is so accustomed to hold the balloting-
pebble, that he awakes with his three fingers
pinched together as if he were offering
incense to the new moon. . . . He is a
merciless judge, never failing to draw the
convicting line and return home with his
nails full of wax like a bumble-bee."

DRAMATIS PERSONAE

Philocleon, an habitual juror
Bdelocleon, son of Philocleon
Sosias and Xanthias, house-servants of Philocleon
Boys, sons of the Chorus
Two Dogs
A Baking-Girl
A Flute-Girl
A Complainant
Chorus of Elders, costumed as Wasps

Wasps

Aristophanes complains (hilariously) of the tendency of Athenians to litigate disputes, and the use of the lawcourts to punish opponents. He again attacks the demagogue Cleon, the "patron true" of lawcourt-haunters.

In the plot, Bdelocleon ("hater-of-Cleon") has an aged father, Philocleon ("lover-of-Cleon") who lives for jury service. Philocleon has especial dedication and delight in convicting the accused and demanding the severest punishment.

The Chorus of Wasps are his fellow enthusiasts ("angry old men with a deadly sting . . . the sting which we use for punishing"). They come for Philocleon early each morning to sally forth to Court. Bdelocleon has tried unsuccessfully to imprison his father in the house, but the avid "lawcourting lover" ingeniously escapes time after time.

Now, the desperate son has cast huge nets over their house and charged two slaves, Xanthias and Sosias, with keeping watch day and night. The desperate father tries climbing through the chimney, but is caught. À la Odysseus with the Cyclops, he clings beneath the belly of an ass in another unsuccessful attempt to slip past them.

The Chorus of Wasps arrive to shout encouragement to him. Fired with the desire "to go with you to the lawcourt and do all the harm I can", old Philocleon applies his practically toothless mouth to the net and somehow manages to gnaw his way through it. Then, following the Wasps' instructions, he ties a rope around him and fastens it to the window from which he nervously descends. Praying to a legendary hero for a safe landing, he swears never to piss or fart near his statue.

His son Bdelocleon awakens and rushes out to stop him from proceeding to Court. Bdelocleon, Xanthius and Sosias engage in a battle royal with the Wasps for possession of Philocleon. (*Bdelocleon.* Strike! Strike! Xanthias! Hit them with your stick. Blind them with smoke!; *Philocleon.* Sting him in the arse!; The Wasps shout "Tyranny!" and threaten them with lawsuits.)

The son, Bdelocleon, calls for a truce, with the argument to be settled by a debate, which they stage. The father claims he and the Wasps are great respected powers in the land, who are well paid, in addition, for their services. His son claims they are duped and short-changed by Cleon and his greedy flatterers.

After a debate royal, Philocleon agrees that his son is right. But he cannot break his addiction to "dispensing justice" -- that is, voting for conviction. Bdelocleon solves this problem by setting up a court in their own household with his father the presiding judge-and-jury.

The first case involves one of their dogs ("a great barker and a licker of dishes"-- i.e. Cleon) accusing another of their dogs of stealing and eating a Sicilian cheese. Poised to condemn the defendant, Philocleon finds himself tricked by his son into voting -- for the first time in his life -- for acquittal.

The old man, overwhelmed by having failed to punish a defendant, gives himself up -- under his son's direction -- to partygoing. He overdoes this too, becoming drunk, disorderly, insolent and then running off with a naked flute-girl. Later, those he has either pummeled or insulted come up to him and threaten to take him to Court. But this seems to inform him how the lawcourts lie in wait for the unwary. It dawns on him that indulgence in wild pleasures is "more worthy and honorable". Now, Philoclean is good-and-cured forever of lawcourt-haunting.

Wasps

Concluding Comment

A feature of Old Comedy, especially Aristophanic Comedy, was the personal relationship between the poet and his audience. Aristophanes took apparent delight in directly addressing his audience via the **parabasis**, a special speech delivered by the Leader of the Chorus.

The Leader of the Chorus of Wasps emitted the following messages from the Poet regarding (1) his outraged disappointment at failing to win first prize the preceding year, and (2) the demagogue Cleon, his sworn enemy.

The poet has a reproach to make against his audience.

He says you have ill-treated him in return for the many services he has rendered you. At first he kept himself in the background and lent help secretly to other poets [evidently meaning the pseudonyms he used in a few earlier plays], and like the prophetic Genius, who hid himself in the belly of Eurycles [an Athenian diviner; he may have been a ventriloquist, as apparently were some priestesses of Apollo who intoned the oracles without moving their lips], slipped within the spirit of another and whispered to him many a comic hit.

Later he ran the risks of the theatre on his own account, with his face uncovered, and dared to guide his Muse unaided.

Though overladen with success and honors more than any of your poets, indeed despite all his glory, he does not yet believe he has attained his goal. His heart is not swollen with pride and he does not seek to seduce the young folk in the wrestling school [i.e. using his renown to sexually seduce young men]. And if any lover runs up to him to complain because he is furious at seeing the object of his passion derided on the stage, he takes no heed of such reproaches, for he is only inspired with honest motives and his Muse is no pander.

From the very outset of his dramatic career he has disdained to assail those who were [mere] men, but with a courage worthy of Heracles himself he attacked the most formidable monsters, and at the beginning went straight for that beast [Cleon] with the sharp teeth, with the terrible eyes that flashed lambent fire like those of Cynna [a contemporary, shameless prostitute] surrounded by a hundred lewd flatterers who spittle-licked him to his heart's content. It [He] had a voice like a roaring torrent, the stench of a seal, the testicles of a foul Lamia [a type of mysterious monster], and the rump of a camel.

Note that Aristophanes is speaking in the amphitheatre to 20,000 people about the most powerful man in the country, and an unscrupulous and belligerent man. To continue with his **parabasis**,

Our poet did not tremble at the sight of this horrible monster, nor did he dream of gaining him over; and again this very day he is fighting for your good.

Last year besides, he attacked those pale, shivering and feverish beings [must refer to informers] who strangled your fathers in the dark, throttled your grandfathers, and who, lying in the beds of the most inoffensive, piled up against them lawsuits, summonses and witnesses to such an extent that many of them flew in terror to the Polemarch for refuge. [The Polemarch was a magistrate who dealt with problems of citizenship. Aristophanes is probably alluding to the many attacks against opponents or intended victims claiming they were not bonafide Athenian citizens. Cleon did this to Aristophanes.]

Such is the champion you have found to purify your country of all its evil, and last year you betrayed him, when he sowed the most novel ideas, which, however, did not strike root, because you did not understand their value.

["Novel ideas" surely signifies his satire on sophists and Socrates (whom he labels a sophist), in *Clouds.* Aristophanes was unhappy that he only received third prize for the effort. I should explain that receiving third prize was still an exceptional achievement, although there were only three contestants. The reason: there may have been hundreds of comedies (a sheer guess on my part) filed for the competition, and only three were selected to be performed.]

Notwithstanding this, he swears by Dionysus, the while offering him libations, that none ever heard better comic verses. It is a disgrace to you not to have caught their drift at once. As for the poet, he is nonetheless appreciated by the enlightened judges. He shivered his oars in rushing boldly forward to board his foe. But in the future, my dear fellow-citizens, love and honor more those of your poets who seek to imagine and express some new thought. Make their ideas your own, keep them in your caskets like sweet-scented fruit. If you do, your clothing will emit an odor of wisdom the whole year through.

CLOUDS 423 BC

This satire on Socrates finds him aloft
in the air seated in a basket, replying
airily and loftily to the protagonist
Strepsiades below:

Socrates. Mortal, what do you want with me?

Strepsiades. First, what are you doing up there?
Tell me, I beseech you.

Socrates (pompously). I am traversing the air
and contemplating the sun.... I have to
suspend my brain and mingle the subtle essence
of my mind with this air, which is of the like
nature, in order clearly to penetrate the things
of heaven. I should have discovered nothing
had I remained on the ground to consider from
below the things that are above.

DRAMATIS PERSONAE

Strepsiades, an elderly farmer
Pheidippides, son of Strepsiades
Servant of Strepsiades
Socrates
Students of Socrates
Right Logic (or Just, Stronger Logic)
Wrong Logic (or Unjust, Weaker Logic)
Pasias, a creditor
Pasias' Witness
Amynias, another creditor
Chaerephon, the philosopher
Chorus of Clouds

Clouds

Clouds, a brilliant, famous and notorious work, spoofs and satirizes Socrates, sophists, and the new scientific learning. Aristophanes evidently considered Socrates a leading representative of sophism, atheism, and the new education. He portrays Socrates as a teacher for pay (contrary to Plato's accounts of the philosopher) in a Thinkery (*Phrontisterion*) inculcating what we call sophistry, plausible but false logic. The Chorus of Clouds symbolize "the mistiness of the new thought". The entire play deals with the pursuit of Wrong, Unjust Logic.

The main character of the piece is not Socrates, although his caricature assumes an essential role. The protagonist is a real 'character', an ironical jester, a devious, bawdy, irreverent actor and malefactor, an artful dodger who eventually gets his comeuppance from *hubris* and his own son. Strepsiades -- that's the old gentleman's name -- signifies a good deal of aged energy and fun.

I happen to be fond of this fellow and, if you have not yet made his acquaintance, let me merrily introduce him to you. Here he comes; I see him now.

Strepsiades goes to Socrates' Thinkery to learn casuistic reasoning in order to swindle his creditors. He has incurred sizable debts due to his son's horse-racing. He hopes to

> learn the nice hair-splittings of subtle Logic
> [and] how one may speak and conquer, right or wrong. [1]

---

[1] (a) "Strepsiades" means "twister", implying the hero's aspiration to deviousness. (See footnote on next page.)

Before encountering Socrates himself, Strepsiades is met by a disciple of the Master. The young man discourses sublimely upon the elevated subject of an insect's 'breaking wind', farting. (this, a rank satire on the new scientific education) The disciple expounds,

> Chaerephon was asking him [Socrates] in turn, which theory did he sanction; that the gnats hummed through their mouth, or backwards, through the tail?
> · He answered thus: the entrail of the gnat is small, and through this narrow pipe the wind rushes with violence straight towards the tail; there, close against the pipe, the hollow rump receives the wind, and whistles to the blast.

That was very impressive, but of little value to the hero in his quest. Then Strepsiades meets Socrates to whom he eagerly exclaims,

> Do let me learn the unjust Logic
> That can shirk debts.

(b) To thoroughly enjoy the play and the character of Strepsiades, I feel that one must temporarily forget, or accept with detachment, Plato's picture of Socrates and the ideal that Socrates represents to us. This may prove difficult, but Aristophanes' achievement in *Clouds* makes the effort worthwhile.

Clouds

Later, pleased with the instruction, Strepsiades brings his son to the school:

> *Strep. (to Socrates).* Give him the knack of
> reasoning down all Justice.

Socrates exits, Right and Wrong Logic entering to hold a debate. Wrong Logic wins it easily, proving that neither Justice nor Truth exists in the world. Both Strepsiades and son Pheidippides have now received instruction in Unjust Logic.

Gleeful about his chances of cheating his creditors, the Twister describes his new self after having mastered the technique of specious reasoning:

> So along with my hide from my duns I escape,
> And to men may appear without conscience or fear.
> Bold, hearty, and wise, a concocter of lies,
> A rattler to speak, a dodger, a sneak,
> A regular claw of the table of law,
> A shuffler complete, well worn in deceit,
> A supple, unprincipled, troublesome cheat.

The Twister proceeds to use false logic with great effect against his creditors. Pheidippides too has learned well his lessons, giving his father a thrashing while logically proving to him the justice of the beating. The play ends when Strepsiades, on the roof, sets fire to the Thinkery.

Concluding Comment

Plato's *Apology* describes the trial of Socrates at which Plato, the great philosopher's great disciple, was present. The Dialogue begins with a speech by the defendant. In this opening speech, Socrates casts blame on comic poets, mentioning Aristophanes by name, for their history of falsely portraying him on the stage. Socrates stated, in part,

> Well, what do my slanderers say? They shall be my prosecutors, and I will sum up their words in an affidavit: 'Socrates is an evil-doer, and a curious person, who searches into things under the earth and in heaven, and he makes the worse appear the better cause; and he teaches the aforesaid doctrines to others.'

> Such is the nature of the accusation. It is just what you have yourselves seen in the comedy of Aristophanes, who has introduced a man whom he calls Socrates, going about and saying that he walks in air, and talking a deal of nonsense concerning matters of which I do not pretend to know either much or little -- not that I mean to speak disparagingly of anyone who is a student of natural philosophy.

Other comic dramatists (e.g. Eupolis) did the like, and Socrates said he found such people "far more dangerous" than his present accusers. They began, he told the jury, "when you were children, and took possession of your minds with their falsehoods."

Clouds

To what extent did Arsitophanes' *Clouds* and other plays contribute to Socrates' predicament? This is difficult to assess, most certainly. I cannot believe that such comedy -- irresistible to the dramatists because their subject was a well-known eccentric -- could have had any significance of an evil nature. One can understand Socrates' irritation, that the merits of gadflyism should go unappreciated. That, instead, he should be joked about and misrepresented as a sophist.

But to be accused of sophism was not a bad thing. The sophists were respected, popular, much sought-after, and commanded good fees. The teaching of rhetoric and eloquence could only thrive in a place like Athens with its popular Assembly and people's lawcourts. Peitho -- the goddess Persuasion -- was a divinity hailed at least as far back as Aeschylus' *Eumenides*. Sophists were **not** hauled into court for teaching people how to present an intrinsically weak argument so effectively that it might prevail over an intrinsically stronger one. They **were** showered with praise and money.

More to the point, Socrates was charged with "impiety" and "corrupting youth" --- two vague, unsubstantiated accusations -- probably because a gadfly was seen as a potentially de-stabilizing force in 399. This was only 5 years after the defeat by Sparta and establishment of the tyranny of the Thirty and a Spartan garrison; 4 years after the dictatorship's overthrow by the forces of democracy (Socrates' chief accuser, Anytus, was one of their generals); and 2 years after an apparently serious threat to attempt a counter-revolution. Government and perhaps populace wanted a lid kept on the usual freedom of expression. They would have wanted Socrates, and everyone else, to stop asking unsettling questions. They may have sought to set an example by prosecuting the most noted questioner of the era.

Again to the point, Socrates conducted the entire trial, including its preface and aftermath, on the basis of high principle. This was fatal. He evidently could have avoided trial, but refused. During the trial itself, he most impoliticly vaunted gadflyism, and scrupulously avoided placating the jurors. Yet the jury vote which convicted him was close, and any type of politic defense would likely have got him off.

Then, after conviction, prosecution and defense offered their proposals for penalty. Here too Socrates stood on suicidal principle, at first insisting that his punishment be the award of free meals in the Prytaneum, those public meals earned by people who had rendered particularly meritorious service to the State.

Finally, when in prison and awaiting the hemlock execution, he was told that his disciples had arranged for his escape. But Socrates refused to escape, no argument or plea impelling him to change his mind.

Why did Socrates become such a stubborn martyr? He gave different reasons at different times for acting throughout as he did. Yet the most convincing reason, in my view, comes from the 3rd century AD biographer, Diogenes Laertius. He related the following apocryphal story:

A friend of Socrates was the most renowned speechwriter of the period, Lysias. He prepared for the philosopher a speech to be delivered at the trial. Socrates rejected it, saying, "A fine speech, Lysias; it is not suitable, however, to me." "If it is a fine speech," rejoined Lysias, "how can it fail to suit you?" "Well," Socrates answered, "would not fine clothes and shoes be just as unsuitable to me?" In other words, it would be excellent rhetorically, but not philosophically correct.

THESMOPHORIAZUSAE   411 BC
(the women who met in assembly
at the Thesmophorion)

Mnesilochus, in female clothing, attends the meeting in order to defend his relative Euripides from the vengeance being contemplated by the assembled, irate women. His dangerous tactic is to attack the female species.

Mnesilochus. Not a single Penelope exists among the women of today, but all without exception are Phaedras.

First Woman. Women, you hear how this creature dares to speak to us.

Mnesilochus. And, Heaven knows, I have not said all that I know. Do you want to hear more?

First Woman. You cannot tell us any more; you have crapped out all you know.

Mnesilochus. I have not told the thousandth part of what we women do. Have I said how we use the hollow handles of our brooms to draw up wine unbeknown to our husbands?

First Woman. The cursed jade!

Mnesilochus. And how we give meats to our pimps at the feast of the Apaturia and then accuse the cat.

First Woman. You're crazy!

Mnesilochus. Have I mentioned the woman who killed her husband with a hatchet? Of another, who caused hers to lose his reason with her potions? And of the Acharnian woman . . .

First woman. Die, you bitch!

DRAMATIS PERSONAE

Euripides
Mnesilochus, Euripides' father-in-law (or elderly kinsman)
Agathon, the tragedian
Servant of Agathon
Chorus attending Agathon
Herald
Women
Cleisthenes (Athens' most publicized homosexual)
A Prytanis (a Member of the Council)
A Scythian Policeman
Chorus of Thesmophoriazusae, women keeping the Feast of
Demeter

Thesmophoriazusae

Aristophanes caricatures tragic poets Euripides and Agathon. The latter (whose plays are lost) catches it for his exquisite ways (reminding of Oscar Wilde's antics during the "aesthetic movement" of the late nineteenth century).

Agathon's servant emerges from the house to intone:

> All people be still!
> Allow not a word from your lips to be heard,
> For the Muses are here, and are making their odes
> In my Master's abodes.
> Let Ether be lulled, and forgetful to blow,
> And the blue sea-waves, let them cease to flow,
> And be noiseless.

Agathon comes out dressed in woman's clothing. He explains his appearance to Euripides and his companion, Mnesilochus ("a garrulous and cheery old man"):

> I choose my dress to suit my poesy.
> A poet, sir, must needs adapt his ways
> To the high thoughts which animate his soul.
> And when he sings of women, he assumes
> A woman's garb, and dons a woman's habits.
> What nature gives us not,
> The human soul aspires to imitate.

Mnesilochus.   Zounds, if I'd seen you when you wrote
the *Satyrs*!

So much for Agathon after that parody. The other poet of the story, Euripides, has a problem about which he seeks Agathon's assistance. "Those women at their Home-fest today", he says, "are going to pay me out for my lampoons" [on woman, depicting them unflatteringly, so claims

Aristophanes]. It is decided that Mnesilochus will be thoroughly shaved and tweezed, dressed as a woman, and thus attend that women's meeting to speak favorably of Euripides.

He does. The meeting proves so stridently, ferociously feminist that his life would be on-the-line if he were discovered. They condemn Euripides to death, and Mnesilochus gamely rises to defend him.

His speech arouses anger, an informer enters to warn the women that a male spy lurks in their midst, and Mnesilochus is uncovered, discovered, and in deadly peril. He takes refuge at an altar, grabs a "baby" from a woman's breast as a hostage (it turns out to be a flask of wine), and awaits Euripides who has sworn to rescue him should the need arise. Eventually he eludes a Scythian policeman set to guard him as Euripides lures the Scythian with a dancing girl.

Thesmophoriazusae

Concluding Comment

One of the characters in the play, Agathon, may have been the most honored tragic poet in Athens after Aeschylus, Sophocles, Euripides. Known for his handsome appearance and innovative talent, he reputedly was the first to consistently devise plot and character without regard for the custom of adapting mythological stories, figures, themes. He took considerable interest in music, and was improvisational here too. Again, here is the misfortune of our losses that fewer than 40 verses remain to us of the dramatist's work.

Agathon won first prize at the Lenaea festival of 416 BC when still a young man under 30. The Lenaea was another festival of Dionysus held in the wintertime. Plato's *Symposium* ("drinking party") was set in Agathon's home where the poet, Socrates, Aristophanes, and others celebrate his triumph in the dramatic competition. Two of Agathon's surviving verses are cited in the Dialogue:

Love gives peace on earth and calms the stormy deep,
Stills the winds and bids the sufferer sleep.

Agathon, like Euripides, went to the court of King Archilaus of Macedon. He also died away from Athens, likewise ending his days in Macedonia. Aristophanes wrote this epitaph in *Frogs* (405 BC):

Hercules. And Agathon, where is he?

Dionysus. Gone far away,
          A poet true, whom many friends miss.

Hercules. Poor fellow! Where?

Dionysus. To feast with peaceful kings.

FROGS 405 BC

"When Euripides came down [here, to Hell], he
gave free exhibitions to our choicest thieves,
footpads, cut-purses, burglars, father-beaters,
-- of whom we have large numbers here; and
when they heard the neat retorts, the fencing,
and the twists, they all went mad and thought
him something splendid. And he, growing
proud, laid hands upon the throne where
Aeschylus sat."

DRAMATIS PERSONAE

Dionysus, god of wine and revel, patron of Drama
Xanthias, servant of Dionysus
Hercules
A Dead Man
Charon, ferryman of the River Styx
Aeacus, doorkeeper of Hades
Maid-Servant of the goddess Persephone
Two Women, Innkeepers
Euripides
Aeschylus
Pluto, god of the underworld
Chorus of Frogs
Chorus of Mystic Initiates

Frogs

The god Dionysus wishes to enter Hades in order to bring back "a genuine poet", Euripides. He and his servant Xanthius visit Hercules to ask the way underground. The muscle-man ought to know since he once descended and brought the three-headed dog Kerberus to earth's surface. Dionysus wears a lion-skin and carries a club - à la Hercules - an outfit he thinks will help them below. The laughing Hercules gives him directions.

Arrived below, Dionysus and Xanthius swap and re-swap the lion-skin and club, depending on Dionysus' appraisal of a friendly or hostile reception. They both are thrashed to see who is the god and who the slave.

At last they get through, encountering Euripides and Aeschylus. Dionysus stages a literary contest between the two poets so as to determine who should be taken back above. Needless to say, given Aristophanes' well-known opinions, Euripides loses and Aeschylus wins.

The author's message: Aeschylus stands for old-fashioned virtues of manly valor and duty; Euripides represents a too-modern skepticism and iconoclasm with his clever subtleties and unheroic heroes.

Concluding Comment

Paganism was undogmatic, tolerant and permissive, often casual, sportive, joyous. Yet it also inspired reverence and awe. Gods and goddesses were worshipped. The holy rituals were solemnly and meticulously performed. Impiety and blasphemy were to be scrupulously avoided.

Remarkably, paradoxically, no sacrilege occurred when placing a god in a starring role in a burlesque comedy. No blasphemy attached to portraying the god -- as in *Frogs*, Dionysus -- behaving ludicrously, getting knocked about in slapstick, even squatting to defecate during which procedure he grunts out a religious phrase.

And this was enacted at a religious festival in honor of Dionysus! The superficial, not genuine contradiction lies in the fact that Dionysus was the god of wine, revel, and fertility. The Great Dionysia included public banqueting. a drinking contest, and the singing of risqué songs. What moderns might deem lewdness was most *apropos* if not *de rigueur* for a fertility-god who was lord of the world's wine.

In Greek paganism, what counted was the **motive** of what many later religionists would be quick to call a blasphemer. Aristophanes' obvious intent was comic. He displays an affection for his Bacchic character, and surely that god on Olympus (or wherever) would look down benevolently and smile on the poet, laughing along with him and his audience in the Theatre of Dionysus.

In matters of religion and sex, the Classical Athenians were refreshingly easy-going and open-minded.

BIRDS   414 BC

A very common fellow presents to
birds the kernel of an uncommon
plan to rectify human affairs.

"The air is between earth and heaven. When
we want to go to Delphi, we ask the Boeotians
for leave of passage. In the same way, as
when men sacrifice to the gods, unless the
gods pay you tribute, you exercise the right of
every nation towards strangers and not allow
the smoke of the sacrifices to pass through
your city and territory. "

DRAMATIS PERSONAE

Euelpides
Pisthetaerus
Epops, the Hoopoe
Trochilus, servant of Epops
Phoenicopterus, a bird
Heralds
A Priest
A Poet
An Oracle-Monger
Meton, a Geometrician
A Commissioner
A Statute-Seller
Iris, a messenger of the gods
A Parricide-Aspirant (that is, he says he wishes to strangle
his father in order to inherit his money)
Kinesias, a Dithyrambic Poet
An Informer
Prometheus, the fire-bearing titan
Poseidon, the god of the sea
Hercules
Triballus, another god, who accompanies Poseidon and
Hercules
A Servant of Pisthetaerus
Messengers
Chorus of Birds

Birds

Two utopian and enterprising Athenians, Pisthetaerus and Euelpides, wish to live peacefully and rationally somewhere in the world. They found CloudCuckooLand, a walled city in the sky which will interdict traffic -- sacrificial offerings -- between gods and men. Birds will thus have a strategic position and rule both deities and mortals -- a far better setup than before. And mankind can live happily everafter, after dealing with a few incidental problems, such as the following results of success:

Herald. Oh you, who have founded so illustrious a city in the air, you know not in what esteem men hold you and how many there are who burn with desire to dwell in it. Before your city was built, all men had a mania for Sparta; long hair and fasting were held in honour, men went dirty like Socrates and carried staves.

Now all is changed. Firstly as soon as it's dawn, they all spring out of bed together to go and seek their food, the same as you do; then they fly off towards the notices and finally devour the decrees.

The bird-madness is so clear that many actually bear the names of birds. There is a halting victualler, who styles himself the partridge; Menippus calls himself the swallow; Opuntius the one-eyed crow; Philocles the lark; Theogenes the fox-goose [et al]. Out of love for the birds they repeat all the songs which concern the swallow, the teal, the goose or the pigeon; in each verse you see wings, or at all events a few feathers.

This is what is happening down there. Finally, there are more than ten thousand folk who are coming here from earth to ask you for feathers and hooked claws; so, mind you supply yourself with wings for the immigrants.

Fortunately, CloudCuckooLand survives the humans' Bird-Mania.

Birds

Concluding Comment

Aristophanes did not like informers. They played a significantly pernicious role in Athenian public affairs. Frequently enough, they might act as false witnesses and suborned accusers, as spies and blackmailers and extortionists. The political use of the lawcourts opened up opportunities if not a career for the unscrupulous and the pliable. The subject populations of Athens' imperialism were particularly vulnerable to Athenian informers' dishonest accusations.

Birds was written during the Sicilian expedition, which would end in disaster for Athens -- a terrible loss of men, ships, and money. Aristophanes refers obliquely to the recall of the brilliant Alcibiades, one of the three generals in charge of the expedition, and the most capable under the circumstances. Informers, evidently working for political opponents of Alcibiades, levelled accusations (to me, incredible) against him of sacrilege. So he was recalled to Athens from the war to face these allegations. (Alcibiades fled to Sparta instead.)

In *Birds,* an informer comes to CloudCuckooLand, and here is the dialogue:

> *Informer.* Where is he who gives out wings to all comers?
> *Pisthetaerus.* Here I am, but you must tell me for what purpose you want them.
> *Informer.* Ask no question. I want wings, and wings I must have.

Pisthetaerus. Do you want to fly straight to the Pellene [an ally of Sparta]?

Informer. I? Why, I am an accuser of the islands, an informer . . .

Pisthetaerus. A fine trade, truly!

Informer. . . . a hatcher of lawsuits. Hence I have great need of wings to prowl round the cities and drag them before justice.

Pisthetaerus. Would you do this better if you had wings?

Informer. No, but I should no longer fear the pirates. I should return with the cranes, loaded with a supply of lawsuits by way of ballast.

Pisthetaerus. So it seems, despite all your youthful vigor, you make it your trade to denounce strangers?

Informer. Well, and why not? I don't know how to dig. (i. e. to work with his hands)

Pisthetearus. But, by Zeus! there are honest ways of gaining a living at your age without all this infamous trickery.

Informer. My friends, I am asking you for wings, not for words.

Pisthetaerus. It's just my words that give you wings.

Informer. And how can you give a man wings with your words?

Pisthetaerus. They all start this way.

Informer. How?

Pisthetaerus. Have you not often heard the father say to young men in the barber shops,

"It's astonishing how Diitrephes' advice has made my son fly to horse-riding" -- "Mine," says another, "has flown towards tragic poetry on the wings of his imagination."

Informer. So that words give wings?

Pisthetaerus. Undoubtedly; words give wings to the mind and make a man soar to heaven. Thus I hope that my wise words will give you wings to fly to some less degrading trade.

Informer. But I do not want to.

Pisthetaerus. What do you reckon on doing then?

Informer. I won't belie my breeding; from generation to generation we have lived by informing. Quick, therefore, give me quickly some light, swift hawk or kestrel wings, so that I may summon the islanders, sustain the accusation here, and haste back there again on flying pinions.

Pisthetaerus. I see. In this way the stranger will be condemned even before he appears.

Informer. That's just it.

Pisthetaerus. And while he is on his way here by sea, you will be flying to the islands to despoil him of his property.

Informer. You've hit it, precisely. I must whirl hither and thither like a perfect humming-top.

Pisthetaerus. I catch the idea. Wait, I've got some fine Corcyraean wings. How do you like them?

Informer. Oh! Woe is me! Why, it's a whip!

Pisthetaerus. No, no. These are the wings, I tell you, that make the top spin.

Informer (*as Pisthetaerus lashes him*). Oh! Oh! Oh!

Pisthetaerus. Take your flight, clear off, you miserable cur, or you will soon see what comes of quibbling and lying. [*The Informer flees.*]

ECCLESIAZUSAE   c. 392 BC
(The Assemblywomen)

Blepyrus. What does this mean? My wife has
vanished! It is nearly daybreak and
she does not return! Ah! What a
damned fool I was to take a wife at
my age, and how I could thrash
myself for having acted so stupidly!
It's a certainty she's not gone out for
any honest purpose. But the thing to
do now is to take a crap.

DRAMATIS PERSONAE

Praxagora, leader of the assemblywomen
Blepyrus, husband of Praxagora
Women
A Man
Chremes, a friend of Blepyrus
Two Citizens
Herald
An Old Man
A Girl
A Young Man
Three Old Hags
A Maid-Servant of Praxagora
Chorus of Women

Ecclesiazusae

Praxagora, a young Athenian woman married to old Blepyrus, dons her sleeping husband's habiliments in the middle of the night and steals out of the house. She lights a lamp as a signal to other women for a pre-arranged meeting. Nothing lewd about her intentions, she wishes to remedy the sad conditions of the State's affairs, and do something about "unworthy ministers". This expounds an old Aristophanic complaint.

The women, who have all dressed as men, attend the morning session of the Assembly with a mind to becoming rulers of the State. (Women, of course, had at this time few if any political rights.) They prevail. Praxagora later describes to her husband a system of Communal Property by which,

> All of all blessings freely partake,
> One life and one system for all men I make.
> The silver, and land, and whatever beside
> Each man shall possess, shall be common and free,
> No marriage or other restraint there will be.

Equality and community of property includes:

> By the side of beauty, so stately and grand,
> The dwarf, the deformed, and the ugly will stand;
> And before you're entitled the beauty to woo,
> You court must pay to the hag and shrew.

Under the new system falls an unfortunate youth. A Willing Maid is eagerly sought by Youth but the young fellow finds himself bedeviled by three hags who, by law, "must come first". The Youth departs miserably, but a banquet ends the play on an optimistic note.

Concluding Comment

Much has been made of *Ecclesiazusae's* possible
relation to Plato's *Republic*. Aristophanes' work had been
written 15 to 20 years **before** Plato's. Critics view with a
touch of horror the thought that Plato might truly have
borrowed some ideas from Aristophanes' comedy about
communism. Was Plato indebted to the burlesquing comic
bard for the conception of community of property as the
foundation for a utopia?

I myself can live with the thought. To start with, extant
literature finds the work of Aristophanes to hold the earliest
examples of utopian designs, of admittedly fanciful but
nonetheless documented schemes for ideal states (*Birds* and
Ecclesiazusae). Why not develop ideas framed comically by
an acknowledged master of mirth and political comment?

Much should be said, however, for the distinct
possibility that the victor over Athens in the Peloponnesian
War provided the major model for both Aristophanes'
Ecclesiazusae and Plato's *Republic*. The intervening years
after Sparta's conquest in 404 BC may have yielded both
dramatist and philosopher time to reflect on the causes of
Athens' defeat. Unquestionably, many Spartan features
appear in Plato's ideal state. And a modified community of
property did exist in the barrack-living life of this military
state. Spartan women, moreover, were far more active in
public than were their counterparts in Athens (*Ecclesiazusae*
and *Lysistrata* notwithstanding).

Interestingly, during the Peloponnesian War itself, a
portion of Athenian youth affected a certain Spartomania.
Aristophanes in *Birds* (414 BC) jests about it:

Ecclesiazusae

Herald. Before your city [in the air] was built,
all men had a mania for Sparta; long hair
and fasting were held in honor, men
went dirty like Socrates and carried
staves. Now all is changed.

THE PLUTUS   388 BC

Chremylus (*to the Plutus, god of wealth*).
Plutus, the most excellent of the gods, come
in here with me. This is the house you must
fill with riches today, by fair means or foul.

Plutus. I don't at all like going into other folks'
houses in this manner; I have never received
any good from it. If I were inside a miser's
house, straightway he would bury me deep
underground. If some honest fellow among
his friends came to ask him for the smallest
coin, he would deny ever having seen me.
Then if I went to a fool's house, he would
sacrifice in dicing and wenching, and very
soon I should be completely stripped and
pitched out of doors.

DRAMATIS PERSONAE

Chremylus, a just man who wants wealth to be distributed
fairly
Cario, servant of Chremylus
Plutus, god of wealth
Blepsidemus, friend of Chremylus
Wife of Chremylus
Lady Poverty
The Good Man
An Informer
An Old Woman
A Youth
Hermes
A Priest of Zeus
Chorus of Rustics

The Plutus

One of the finest comedies I have ever read, *The Plutus* satirizes in burlesque style the human love of Money. It was Aristophanes' most popular play in ancient times and in the Renaissance, preserved in 148 manuscripts -- which is astounding.

The story recounts how the conscientious Chremylus wishes the blind god of wealth, the Plutus, to stop blindly distributing his riches to good and bad people alike (usually to the latter). Chremylus sends the Plutus, accompanied by Chremylus' servant Cario (who has been systematically stealing from his master for years), to the divine physician Asclepius for treatment. Cured of his blindness, the good-hearted Plutus comes to live in the Chremylus household, passing around his wealth only to people he sees are good.

One of those to visit the Plutus to offer thanks is the Good Man. Here is his story:

> *Good Man.* I am come to thank the God:
> great blessing hath he wrought for me. For I,
> inheriting a fair estate [before Plutus was
> cured of blindness], used it to help my
> comrades in their need, esteeming that the
> wisest thing to do.
> *Cario.* I guess your money soon began to fail.
> *Good Man.* Aye, that it did!
> *Cario.* And then you came to grief.
> *Good Man.* Aye, that I did! And I supposed that
> they, whom I had assisted in their need,
> would now be glad to help me when in need
> myself. But all slipped off as though they
> saw me not.

.I wish to relate something more about the Good Man. He has been made wealthy again, thanks to the Plutus. For many long years after his impoverishment, he had worn the same cloak and pair of shoes.

> *Good Man.* I come with thankfulness to praise
> the God.
> *Cario.* But what's the meaning, by the Powers,
> of that, that ancient cloak your boy is bearing?
> *Good Man.* This too I bring, an offering to the
> God.
> *Cario.* That's not the robe you were initiate in?
> *Good Man.* No, but I shivered thirteen years
> therein.
> *Cario.* Those shoes?
> *Good Man.* Have weathered many a storm
> with me.
> *Cario.* And them you bring as votive offerings?
> *Good Man.* Yes.   (848)

The Good Man attaches sentimental value to those ancient shoes and cloak. What better offering could he make?

People like the Good Man are grateful for the Plutus' benevolence, but others such as the Informer complain of having been impoverished. An interesting complaint comes from Lady Poverty who engages in a heated debate with Chremylus, she claiming that human beings are better off poor than rich. (The lady may have the better of the argument.) Another complainant, Old Lady, bemoans the loss of her devoted young boyfriend (that is, dedicated to her cakes and ale).

Hermes, the god of thieves -- Cario and Hermes recognize one another instantly -- also has a complaint:

nobody now sacrifices food and goodies to him seeking for a return on the investment. Hermes wants to live in Chremylus' house where the food is, and he does.

Zeus eventually moves in too. When this happens, the Plutus can go back to the Treasury on the Acropolis. After all, when Zeus -- Righteousness -- inhabits the human world, there is no need for Wealth to set things right.

The Plutus is a wonderful philosophic comedy.

Concluding Comment

As previously mentioned, *The Plutus* was a popular play in the later ancient world, in the Middle Ages, and in the Renaissance. It was preserved in an astounding 148 manuscripts.

Modern critics, however, have little regard for the comedy. I personally cannot fathom the modern opinion, and give it no credit. I most highly recommend that the reader of these lines spend the time to read *The Plutus* and arrive at his/her own opinion.

Conclusion

ARISTOPHANES -- The humor and intelligence characteristic of Aristophanic poetic drama do not tell the whole story of his Art. Like the tragedians, especially Aeschylus and Euripides, he was writing out of a sense of Social Conscience and communicating with his audience about socio-political matters of the utmost importance to the city-state, the beloved **polis**.

A critic and reformer, Aristophanes did with plot and poetry and bawdy jests what Pericles and Themistocles and Miltiades had done in their own governmental and military fields of endeavor. The Graces did right well when they gathered in the soul of Aristophanes.

Greek Drama: Conclusion

Imagine such a magnificent tradition of Tragedy and Comedy occurring 2,500 years ago at the very dawn of Western civilization! It is a dire judgment on our times that we have steadily lost contact with this Tradition.

We need to return Aeschylus, Sophocles, Euripides, and Aristophanes to our educational systems and to our personal reading experiences. Our intellectual and moral cultures rue the loss and insist upon a renewed acquaintance. Our emotional lives -- so much at the mercy of modern emptiness and distortion -- begs for the poetic and philosophic beauties of the Classical achievement of Greek Drama.

We require a Modern Renaissance, and re-acquiring a knowledge of Greek Tragedy and Comedy would offer a valuable start in that Olympian direction.

Glossary of Deities and Heroes

Aias (Latin, Ajax)
Aphrodite (Latin, Venus)
Apollo (Latin, Apollo)
Ares (Latin, Mars)
Artemis (Latin, Diana)
Asclepius (Latin, Aesculapius)
Athena (or, Pallas Athena; Latin, Minerva)
Cronus (Latin, Saturn)
Demeter (Latin, Ceres)
Dionysus (Latin, Bacchus)
Hephaestus (Latin, Vulcan)
Hera (Latin, Juno)
Heracles (Latin, Hercules)
Iocasta (Latin, Jocasta)
Hermes (Latin, Mercury)
Odysseus (Latin, Ulysses)
Persephone (Latin, Proserpina)
Polydeuces (Latin, Pollux)
Poseidon (Latin, Neptune)
Zeus (Latin, Jupiter, Jove)

Note: The Greeks called Greece "Hellas" and themselves "Hellenes".

Index

A

Achilles, 45, 47, 71, 113, 114, 115, 116, 145, 146, 151, 153, 166, 167, 169, 171, 214, 215
Acropolis, 4, 29, 243, 256, 257, 258, 311
Admetus, 226, 227, 228, 229
Adrastus, 184, 185
Aegeus, 128, 221
Aegisthus, 44, 45, 46, 50, 51, 102, 103, 160, 162, 164
Aeneas, 144, 145
Agathon, 284, 285, 287
Agave, 132, 134
Agora, 4, 246
Agoracritus (the Sausage-Seller), 260
Alcibiades, 297
Alcmene, 200
Amazons, 139
Anaxagoras, 120
Antisthenes, 181
Anytus, 279
Aphrodite (Latin, Venus), 107, 138, 141, 318
Apollo, 4, 39, 51, 55, 56, 57, 58, 80, 81, 84, 121, 161, 173, 183, 208, 209, 220, 221, 226, 228, 269, 318
Apology of Plato, 278
Areopagus court, 57
Ares (Latin, Mars), 31, 318
Argos, 20, 21, 22, 31, 44, 45, 49, 50, 73, 160, 167, 184, 185, 186, 192, 209
Aristotle, 66, 79, 173, 223

Artemis (Latin, Diana), 138, 139, 141, 167, 168, 171, 172, 174, 318
Asclepius, 309, 318
Assembly (Ecclesia), 28, 243, 245, 246, 262, 279, 303
Athena, 56, 57, 70, 71, 144, 146, 150, 172, 184, 186, 187, 220, 258, 318
Atossa, 24, 25
Atreus, 45, 51, 165

B

Babylonians of Aristophanes, 263
Bdelocleon, 266, 267, 268
Blepyrus, 301, 302, 303
Brasidas, 253

C

Cadmus, 132
Calchas, 45, 167, 168
Cario, 308, 309, 310, 311
Cassandra, 44, 45, 46, 149, 150
Castor, 160, 161, 204
Chaerephon, 274, 276
Chremes, 302
Chremylus, 307, 309, 310, 311
Cleisthenes, 284
Cleon, 157, 240, 241, 251, 253, 260, 261, 262, 263, 267, 268, 269, 270, 271
Cleonymus, 250, 251

CloudCuckooLand, 295, 296
Clytemnestra, 16, 44, 45, 46, 47,
   50, 51, 52, 102, 103, 105, 160,
   161, 166, 167, 168, 172, 208
Crassus, 135, 136
Creon, 33, 67, 71, 78, 79, 80, 90,
   91, 92, 95, 96, 97, 98, 99, 128,
   178, 184, 185, 200, 201
Crete, 202
Creusa, 220, 221

D

Danaus, 20, 21
Darius, 14, 24, 25
Deianeira, 67, 107, 108, 109, 110
Delian League, 221
Delphi, 55, 57, 81, 121, 175, 215,
   220, 221, 293
Delphic Oracle, 4, 80, 91, 139
Demophon, 192
democracy, 10, 14, 15, 17, 27, 60,
   185, 188, 201, 246, 279
Demos, 259, 260, 261
Demosthenes
   (the contemporary general, not
      the 4th century BC orator and
      statesman), 260
deus ex machina, 116, 186, 209,
   211, 215
Dicaeopolis, 244, 245, 246, 251
Diogenes Laertius, 280
Diomedes, 144, 146
Dionysian festival, 14, 222, 235
Dionysus (Latin, Bacchus), 22,
   131, 132, 133, 271, 287, 288,
   290, 291, 292, 318
Dioscuri, 160, 204
Dolon, 143, 144, 145, 146, 245

E

Ecclesia (Assembly), 246
Egyptians, 21
Eleusis, 14
Elpinice, 197, 198
Eteocles, 31, 32, 33, 34, 91, 97,
   177, 178, 181, 185
Euelpides, 294, 295
Eupolis, 251, 278
Eurystheus, 192
Evadne, 184, 186

F

Fate, 39, 61, 109
Flatterers of Eupolis, 251

G

Ghost of Clytemnestra, 56, 57, 58
Ghost of Darius, 25
Ghost of Polydore, 152
Good Man, 308, 309
Great Dionysia, 22, 251, 253, 292
Guard in Sophocles' *Antigone*, 97

H

Haemon, 96, 98, 99
Hamlet, 79, 139, 153
Hector, 115, 143, 144, 145, 146,
   150, 153, 213, 214, 215
Helen of Troy, 45, 57, 62, 121,
   144, 150, 151, 153, 167, 203,
   204, 205, 206, 208, 209, 214,
   215
Hephaestus (Latin, Vulcan), 36,
   37, 318
Hera (Latin, Juno), 38, 201, 318

Myron Stagman

The BURLESQUE COMEDIES of ARISTOPHANES

Detailed storylines, with choice morsels of dialogue, of all 11 surviving plays of Classical Athens' comic genius

The champion of
no-holds-barred
satire on Politics
and People

Background Essays
on Life in
Ancient Athens:
Democracy
Slavery
Sex
God
War

Bawdy
Rollicking
Cutting

Fighting for
Peace &
a healthy
Sex Life

an education
in genuine
Democracy

MYRON STAGMAN

GUIDE TO SHAKESPEARE

storylines   highlights   deeper meanings

for all of Shakespeare's 38 plays

Antony and Cleopatra
Romeo and Juliet
Titus Andronicus
Timon of Athens
Julius Caesar
Coriolanus
King Lear
Macbeth
Othello
Hamlet

Midsummer Night's Dream
Much Ado About Nothing
Merry Wives of Windsor
Taming of the Shrew
Merchant of Venice
Comedy of Errors
As You Like It
Twelfth Night
Winter's Tale
Cymbeline

King John
Richard III
Richard II
1 Henry IV
II Henry IV
Henry V
Henry VI
Henry VIII

Pericles
The Tempest
Troilus and Cressida
Two Noble Kinsmen
Love's Labour's Lost
Measure for Measure
All's Well That Ends Well
Two Gentlemen of Verona